SO, YOUR WIFE LEFT YOU...
NOW WHAT?

*A Clinical Psychologist's Guide to
Life, Sex, and Dating Post-Divorce*

By Dr. Elana Hoffman

Edited by Lil Barcaski

Published by: GWN Publishing
www.GWNPublishing.com

Cover Design: Kristina Conatser

Custom photography by Elliott O'Donovan

ISBN: 978-1-965971-04-8

DEDICATION

To my past, current, and future clients.
Thank you for your trust, vulnerability,
openness, and humor. I'm always learning
from you. I am truly honored to be the re-
cipient of your authenticity and humanity.

TABLE OF CONTENTS

FOREWORD

Navigating life after a separation from your spouse can be overwhelming. As a family law attorney for over 25 years, I have seen many of my clients struggle to understand what went wrong in their marriages, and more importantly what they can do differently when moving forward. Dr. Hoffman's book is a comprehensive guide for men going through this difficult transition process, including easily digestible tips for dealing with the feelings and challenges that inevitably arise as part of the divorce. She offers a concise explanation of the various options for therapy that are available, as well as very clear and direct dating advice. In a light-hearted and funny manner, she provides practical strategies for developing emotional intelligence and becoming a more in-tuned partner in future relationships. As devastating as divorce can be, it is an incredible opportunity to learn about your own needs and wants, while also building better ways to connect with others and develop deeper and more meaningful bonds. This book will undoubtedly help may overcome the disappointment they experienced during the demise of their marriage and move on to a better place. I will definitely encourage my male clients to read this book.

Regina A. DeMeo, JD. Principal at the Markham Law Firm in Bethesda, MD, formerly an adjunct professor at the Family Justice Center for George Washington University Law School in Washington, D.C.

Since 2010, Regina she has been a frequent guest lecturer and presenter in various universities, as well as on radio, tv, and numerous podcasts. After being featured in the Washington Post, she became the host of MMCTV's show Making it Last for two years, and she was a frequent legal commentator for Sirius XM in 2012. In July 2013 she appeared on Good Morning America, and published a children's book, Gina the Gymnast. *Her goal is to minimize the trauma in a divorce, protect children and promote healthy relationships. By focusing on settlement negotiations and alternative dispute resolution, including mediation and Collaborative Divorce, litigation is usually the option of last resort for her clients. She has served on the Boards of the Women's Bar Association of DC, the Women Business Owners of Montgomery County and Collaborative Divorce Association in MD. From 2019-2020 she was an adjunct professor for the George Washington University Family Justice Center. Numerous publications have quoted her, and she has published several articles throughout her career. As a result, throughout the years, she has been recognized by Washingtonian, Bethesda Magazine, and Super Lawyers Magazine as one of the top family law attorneys in the DC Area.*

ENDORSEMENTS

"*So Your Wife Left You, Now What?* is a wonderful, entertaining and highly readable book for men navigating the end of a relationship. It has page-after-page of practical tools and meaningful insights on how to build a healthy and happy life post-divorce. When your "happily-ever-after" didn't go as planned, this book is an invaluable resource. I would highly recommend this book to all my clients and colleagues. Dr. Elana Hoffman is nothing short of a national treasure."

—James J. Sexton, Esq., Law Offices of James J. Sexton, P.C.

"This book offers a transformative experience through clear guidance and practical strategies designed for men seeking personal growth and positive change after a divorce. Dr. Hoffman blends authentic and humorous insight with effective clinical strategies that empower the reader to navigate the turbulent waters of divorce. A must read for cisgendered heterosexual men looking to turn a painful experience into a journey of self-awareness and interpersonal successes. I wouldn't hesitate to recommend this book to clients and colleagues."

—Dr. Korrin Saunders, Clinical Psychologist in Private Practice

"In my therapy practice, I work with many men navigating problems in their relationships, who struggle with where to start, especially during and after a divorce. Dr. Hoffman's book for divorced men is a fantastic resource that I will be recommending to these clients in the future. The topics are covered in an easily digestible way, including for those without much or any therapy experience. Many people will have a friend or family member go through a divorce, want to help, but not know exactly how. Buying this book as a gift, combined with an offer of a listening ear and spending time together is a winning combination to be there for the divorced men in your life."

—Dr. CJ Seitz-Brown, Clinical Psychologist in Private Practice

"This book is a treasure chest for men in the early stages of divorce. The friendly, upbeat and totally accessible way the book is written left me hanging on to every single word. I love the author's honest and accurate approach to providing guidance and inspiration during this challenging period of life. I particularly resonate with her encouragement towards an uncontested divorce and the useful tools to understand how to navigate the dating world to show up wiser, healthier and more balanced than before. I'm delighted to pass this invaluable resource forward to friends and clients."

—Natasha Esther Zara, break up and relationship coach and co-founder of Happily Divorced (Instagram at @trustingtheway and @happilydivorce)

INTRODUCTION

Okay, gentleman, you've taken the first step. You either bought this book yourself (impressive if so, it shows you are doing the emotional work!) or you took someone's recommendation seriously enough to at least open it (if you are a friend, family member, or client of mine who bought a copy, many thanks). Before we get into it, I want to be clear about something. I don't intend to patronize you, and I surely am not a man-hater. I'm writing this because I've talked to a lot of men who are going through or who have recently gone through a divorce, and I know it can be an incredibly hard time, especially if it was unexpected. Divorce is still often seen as a failure, and one thing I hope to convey in this book is that it is not! It is an opportunity for hindsight and reflection, to learn from your marriage (and other previous experiences), and to take all that knowledge, move forward, and live a rewarding and valued life. Like many things that don't go as planned in life, it is an opportunity for something new to come your way.

I am a Clinical Psychologist who specializes in relationships. I see individuals and couples in my telehealth private practice from my home in Washington D.C. I have learned so much from my experience that I wanted to share this to a broader audience. In this book, I talk about my experience in general and what I see in my practice: Details of any specifics have, of course, been changed.

In addition to my professional experience having a front-row seat to the ups and downs of relationships and the general human experience, I have a family legacy of divorce, which also well equips me to write on this topic—as well as being divorced and a parent myself. I suppose this is what got me interested in psychology in the first place; I wanted to understand my own family patterns. That, combined with a keen interest in my psychology classes starting in high school, led me to pursue my Ph.D. in Clinical Psychology, with a current focus on relationships. My professional interests dovetail nicely with my longstanding fascination with relationships in general, as evidenced by my interest in *Love is Blind*, *The Bachelor*, and so on. I follow all kinds of relationship content on social media. I have many recommendations (see list in the back of the book), and when I reconnect with friends that have known me a long time and I tell them what I do, they all say something like, "Duh, you were always going to be a Psychologist specializing in relationships."

I feel incredibly lucky to do what I do! My graduate and post-doctoral training is in addiction and trauma, and I certainly use this lens and background in my work today. I have learned a ton about the impact of relationship satisfaction on mental health. In my view and experience, this is the driver of so many of our maladaptive behaviors. Anxiety, depression, low self-esteem, substance use, suicidal ideation, suicide completions (sadly), etc., so often are byproducts of unhealthy relationships. Now, of course, everyone brings in their own issues, and things are very often bidirectional, but I often see people get much healthier when their relationships improve or people decide a relationship isn't for them. I have learned that looking at relationships as a factor for someone's mental health is imperative, which is why I decided to focus my practice on relationships (couples, individuals, and all kinds of relationship configurations). We are all human, and we all want love and intimacy. Relationship satisfaction is a huge predictor of life satisfaction; in fact, the longest running study (85 years!) on relationships published in 2023 by Harvard confirms that positive relationships, more than any other variable (i.e. money, career achievement, exercise, healthy diet) keep us happier, healthier, and living longer.

I also wanted to write on this topic because I see a huge gap in therapy and education when it comes to sex and other forms of intimacy. My personal background as well as my professional experience with all kinds of people and relationships position me well to share my pearls of wisdom with you, dear readers. Although my practice is diverse in terms of sexual orientation, gender identity, race, religion, ethnicity, etc., my main audience for this book is cisgender men who are dating women. This book is intended for men who are relatively early in the process of separating/divorcing. I use the terminology "ex-wife" and "wife" interchangeably throughout the book, because your divorce might not be official.

I was also motivated by this topic because I have spoken with so many men who are floundering during this period of time. Of course you are! If you are in the majority of men, you did not initiate the divorce. Seventy percent of divorces are initiated by women. You are likely not only feeling lost, but I'm sure your self-esteem and confidence have taken a bit of a hit. You might have a lot of questions as well. I have also met people who are on the other side of this incredibly difficult time and have learned a lot from them too! My hope with this book is not only to make you feel understood, but to engender a sense of hope for the rest of your life. Although you did not choose this and you might have even pleaded or prayed (if that's your jam) for it not to happen, there are so many opportunities here that you have yet to see.

I want to help you self-reflect and introspect about what went wrong in your marriage, give you possible insights into why you were drawn to a person who was ultimately not a good fit for you, as well as gain confidence that you can handle this next chapter and come out the other side even better! Although this book is not a substitute for a good therapist, it will hopefully at least give you some things to think about and some tools from someone who sees a lot of the struggles that men deal with and is compassionate to them. When I see men build their confidence, it is truly transformative. This is not the end of your life; it is really the beginning.

The most common reaction people get when they say they are getting divorced or are divorced is "I'm sorry." I wish this was not the go-to sentiment. You have the opportunity for a new life. We have a short time on this planet, and no one should be miserable. If you don't believe that last statement, this likely has something to do with your upbringing. More on that later. Marriage, despite what we are told by cultural and societal norms, not to mention religious institutions, family, etc., is NOT the be-all-end-all, especially not an unhappy one.

Statistically speaking, you will likely remarry. Remarriage rates are lower than they used to be, and declining 50% from 1990 to 2019 (Reynolds, 2021). However, according to data from the National Survey of Family Growth, 52% of divorced men and 44% of divorced women will get remarried within five years after divorce. You will likely remarry someone who has also been divorced, however; the rates of divorce increase with each subsequent marriage (60% and 73% for second and third marriages, respectively). If you decide to remarry, the hope is you will have a 2.0, and be happier than you could have imagined. I'd like to give you some tools to engender self-reflection and growth, so you are in the best position for that to happen. Ultimately, you have the gift of freedom to reflect and grow, and I hope it is used well.

The chapters in this book are essentially all bite-sized versions of much bigger topics. Not all of them will apply to you, so feel free to take what is useful and leave the rest. For example, if you already have good legal representation, you can skip that chapter. However, I encourage reading most of it to help develop your introspection and self-awareness. That is truly the foundation for change, though meaningful change, of course, also requires changing your behaviors.

Many of the chapters have homework assignments, and some of those involve deep introspection about the topic discussed! Yes, this is a crucial starting point, even though that doesn't seem like a tangible "to-do." Some chapters also have "to-do" items. The people who will benefit from this book are those of you who WANT to self-reflect, grow, recognize your own contributions to your patterns, and use that newfound insight and understanding to move forward and do things differently. If you do not want to introspect about your family of origin and your upbringing, this book is also likely not for you. Again, though this book is not therapy, it is written for those of you who are or want to become more psychologically-minded and introspective.

Another quick warning/caveat of this book. I am a die-hard *Sex and the City* (SATC) fan, and despite it being dated in many ways, I still find it quite relevant and relatable. If you are reading this, you are probably familiar, though I am not sure to what degree.

There are a lot of lessons to be learned from the show, and I often suggest that my male clients watch the original series if they haven't seen it. It is an excellent window into the minds and hearts of 30-something successful, beautiful, smart, and funny women who are navigating the dating market. As a man dating women, it could be very informative for you.

First lesson in this book: Be open-minded. You never know what you can learn! Also, consider yourself warned that I open every chapter with a SATC quote and I relate it to the topic. As a quick refresher, the main characters are: Carrie, Miranda, Samantha, and Charlotte. Please don't give up on me just yet, it'll be useful, I promise. And, it is essentially just an extension of my everyday life, where I am basically quoting it and referring to it constantly. So, have faith and read on!!

CHAPTER 1

SHE SAYS I'M EMOTIONLESS

Naming and Understanding Your Emotions

"You know, being scared is not an easy thing for a man to admit." —SAMANTHA

"So what? They get a medal for correctly identifying a feeling?? We do that all day long! I feel pissed off! Ta-da!" —MIRANDA

I love this quote because, despite it being slightly anti-male, it does emphasize the importance of being fully aware of your emotions. In this example, Samantha was referring to Richard, her boss and ex-boyfriend with whom she had a brief relationship that ended with her walking in on him going down on another woman. In this conversation, she is telling the girls she got back together with him because he "admitted" he was scared about his strong feelings for her, which is why he cheated. If we are to believe Richard, the lesson here is pretty clear: Be aware of your emotions and communicate them! He hurt Samantha very much because of his actions, which seemingly stemmed from lack of self-awareness (giving the benefit of the doubt here). Spoiler alert: This relationship did not work out.

Self-awareness—a huge part of which is awareness of your internal emotional state—is where it starts, my friends.

IT'S OK TO BE SAD!

It is also ok to be mad, scared, uncertain, anxious, ashamed, and so on. At this stage, I think you are probably having some "big feelings," ones that you might be pushing down. You might be tempted to numb your feelings with some unhelpful coping mechanisms like alcohol, weed, other drugs, porn, sex, gambling, etc. If you are in the majority of men, you are not the spouse that initiated this divorce, and might have been blindsided by it (though there were likely flags that things were falling apart but more on that later). You may have even begged your wife not to leave. You may have offered (and even tried) couple's therapy, expensive vacations, gifts, and probably more. At this point, you probably think your life is over. Au contraire! Though it is super important to be able to sit with these really intense feelings that come up during this time, I am also here to inspire optimism that this is not the end of your life, and is in fact the opposite! It is just the beginning (so cliché, I know, I know!) But I promise, you have a real opportunity if you choose to see it that way, and it is my hope that you will start to see that perspective by reading this book.

THE GRIEF CYCLE

A lot has been written about the 5 stages of grief, which is a model originally introduced by Elizabeth Kubler-Ross in her book *On Death and Dying*. Although divorce is not a death per se (and in fact I am trying to get you to look at it in the exact opposite light), it is definitely a loss and a major change, and one where a person is susceptible to a similar process of grieving. The stages outlined by Kubler-Ross are as follows: Denial, Anger, Bargaining, Depression, and Acceptance. In the denial phase, a person thinks the event is a mistake, and they might cling to a false reality that the event is not happening. In divorce, this might look like not taking steps to move the process along, not talking to your kids about it, not telling friends and family, etc.

The next stage, anger, might look like "why me," blaming someone else, etc. This "phase" CAN last a long time in divorce. I have seen clients who have been married to someone else for decades and are still angry at their first ex-wife for leaving them. The third phase, bargaining, is especially applicable to divorce and was mentioned above. In this phase, the person grieving negotiates in order to make the event not happen. So begging, pleading, promising change, etc., are all part of this phase. Depression is next and is often just that. Sadness, listlessness, "what is the point?" Drinking and negative thoughts such as "I'll never find love again" might enter one's mind during this time. The final stage is acceptance. In this phase, you accept the event fully, with all the thoughts and feelings that come along with it. Without accepting divorce, and all its ramifications (positive and negative), you can't begin to live your life.

In my experience, these stages are not discreet stages, and people cycle in and out of all of them at some point during and after divorce. Even people years out can be sad about their divorce sometimes, even if they have accepted it at one point. This is why it is so important to recognize and sit with the feelings, because you can't really rush them. Acceptance is a process that people go in and out of with most loses, from what I have seen. So don't beat yourself up if you thought you were past anger or sadness, and you feel those emotions sometimes. Especially if you need to co-parent, that is likely going to happen. It doesn't mean you haven't accepted the situation.

ACCEPTANCE OF EMOTIONS

You may have heard the phrase, "don't let divorce define you." I actually think this sentiment is fairly unhelpful. In some ways, it is pushing away acceptance of your situation. Of course, being divorced is not the ONLY thing that defines you, but I wish it was more widely accepted as not-the-absolute-worst-thing-in-the-world. A client of mine told me a story about how she ran into a friend of hers very early in her separation, and when she updated her friend about her life, she was met with an enthusiastic "Congratulations!" She told me it was something she didn't know she needed to hear. Although it sounds crazy to respond to a divorce with that sentiment, hear me out. Cultural, familial, and religious pressure still promote heterosexual marriage as the be all, end all, happily ever after, tax breaks and all. We are essentially brainwashed to think that this is the right path, and anything that deviates is cause for "I'm sorrys." Lyz Lenz in her book, *This American Ex-Wife*, discusses this idea in great detail if you are interested. The sentiment behind the "congratulations" really means: you are starting a new chapter in your life, and THAT is worth celebrating, not pitying. At the same time, of course it is sad things did not work out the way you had planned/wanted them to. Divorce is not something to be cavalier about, make no mistake, and I understand you might be a ways from thinking about this as a positive thing. For now, just know that whatever you are feeling is acceptable!

Grief, anger, sadness, loneliness... it's all okay! We are taught from a young age these tough emotions are "bad." But really, they just ARE. We have primary emotions hardwired into us.

There is some debate about which emotions are classified as "primary," but often these include anger, sadness, fear, joy, surprise, love, and disgust. We have all evolved with these emotions because they serve a purpose! They all communicate something very important to us and the people around us. Fear motivates us to assess for danger. Anger calls us to action. Sadness tells us and the people around us we need support. Joy/love connects us. We simply cannot survive as a species without these emotions and the important messages they convey. For a slightly simplistic, yet cute, primer on these ideas, go see Inside Out and Inside Out 2. Facial expressions, body language, etc., are all reflections of our emotions and crucial to our evolution. When we label them as "bad," we just automatically discount them. Many of these emotions (intense anger, grief, loneliness) are indeed unpleasant. But they are a normal part of the human experience, and the more we suppress them, the more they come back in unhealthy ways (outbursts, substance use, stonewalling, vitriol, violence, and so forth.). A lot of men I see in my practice fit the stereotype that men think more logically, rather than emotionally. A lot of times they tell me that emotions get in the way, and they are a nuisance. Clients often talk about how they don't want to make decisions with their emotions; for example: ending relationships. To this I say, we do that all the time, it is just not always in our conscious awareness. We often pursue romantic connections in large part because of love or lust, for example. Emotions simply cannot be discounted. Logic and facts are also important, of course. BOTH are.

WISE MIND

There is a term for this in fact. "Wise mind" is a term used in Dialectical Behavioral Therapy (DBT, more on that and therapy in general in the next chapter). "Wise mind" is the synthesis of "emotion mind" (think hot, intense, red) and "reasonable mind" (think cold, blue, facts, logic). "Wise mind" is the "middle path." Picture a Venn diagram with wise mind in the middle. This concept honors the notion that BOTH are important in decision-making. If we only make decisions using either emotion mind or reasonable mind, we are leaving out super important information! Let's say you are at the grocery store, and your cart reflects only reasonable mind. What is in your cart? Probably all very healthy and reasonably priced items and maybe nothing that brings you joy. What about emotion mind? Well, I know what my cart would look like. Both are actually important! Everyone has a "wise mind" or an inner wisdom. Keep this concept in mind.

EMOTIONS AS WAVES

The other thing about intense emotions, they pass. We are not wired to feel level ten rage or heartbreak for an extended period of time. This comes in waves. If we actually let ourselves FEEL our emotions, they will pass. The wave will subside. It might come back. It'll subside again. Think of it like a soda bottle. If you shake a soda bottle and leave the top on, the next time you open it, it will explode. But if you open it a little at a time and let some fizz out, it is easier to contain, and it won't explode all over the place. This is what has to be done with your emotions during this time. Let them out slowly as they arise. They won't kill you. That's the thing. We often think—mostly because we are taught—that we can't handle these emotions, "don't cry," "it's okay," etc. Men especially. This is what is referred to as "toxic masculinity." The idea that men who show their emotions are weak. This truly could not be further from the truth. Not only is this a harmful trope for men to buy into because it leads to avoidance of their emotions, but women actually want men who are aware of and sensitive to their own emotions (especially after divorce, when many women are looking for more sensitive men because their first husbands might not have been). So, learning how to identify and sit with tough emotions is going to help you immensely during this time. A trained therapist can help you with this and help you learn how to express them in helpful ways (more on therapy in a later chapter). For now, pay attention to everything happening in your mind and your body when you are feeling these emotions. This is called mindfulness. Present-moment awareness of what you are feeling. Are you tense, are you crying, is your heart racing, etc.? Present-moment awareness leads to emotion identification. If you have had a hard time regulating your emotions (or your ex-wife or anyone else in your life has suggested this might be the case), there are therapy programs designed for this (again, more on this later). For now, I just want to give you permission to feel however it is that you feel.

TL;DR

- It's ok to be sad (and angry, scared, hurt, disappointed, lonely, etc.).
- "Bad" feelings are human feelings.
- "Wise Mind" is the synthesis of emotion mind and reasonable mind, and is super important! We all have an inner wisdom to channel.
- Pushing away your emotions doesn't work; they just come back in unhealthy/unproductive ways.
- Mindfulness is key to sitting with uncomfortable/ unpleasant emotions.

HOMEWORK

☐ Practice sitting with your emotions and noticing what is going on in your body.

☐ Give yourself permission to feel your emotions; notice the labels and judgements that come up.

☐ Consider journaling your emotions! You can buy specific journals for this. Google away!

CHAPTER 2

I SHOULD PROBABLY GET A LAWYER

A Brief Guide to the Legal Process

""Charlotte York was a wonderful wife, stop. She did nothing wrong, stop. Give her everything she wants, stop. Seriously mother, STOP." —HARRY GOLDENBLATT, reading a telegram from Trey McDougal

This storyline is maybe one of my favorites from the show. In this scene, Charlotte is in divorce proceedings with her lawyer, Harry Goldenblatt and her soon-to-be-ex mother-in-law, Bunny McDougal and her counsel. They are fighting over the apartment Charlotte and her soon-to-be ex-husband, Trey McDougal lived in together. Trey had verbally given Charlotte the apartment, but his mother, Bunny (a recurring thorn in Charlotte's side) disagreed with Trey and involved herself in a legal battle. In the above quote, Harry is reading a telegram that Trey had sent to the office to settle the debate over the apartment. This telegram prompted Bunny to comply and solidified Charlotte's divorce which ultimately led to her to fall in love with her lawyer, Harry. I'm pretty sure this happens more often than we hear about, and I'm not totally sure what the ethics are around it... Anyone a lawyer and can tell me?? Either way, they are truly an example of a loving second marriage, though if Charlotte were my client I would encourage her to think through whether she was rushing into something so soon after divorce. However, she and Trey were mismatched from the beginning (they got married in about five seconds and had a lot of sexual issues), and she initiated the divorce because they disagreed about pursuing parenthood when they had trouble conceiving, so perhaps in this case she was ready soon after.

Anyway! Back to you. This chapter is an overview about the legal process, sans falling in love with and marrying your divorce lawyer. Though I will say, Harry Goldenblatt is husband goals. If you are watching the series, pay attention to how he treats Charlotte.

A lot of people don't fully grasp that a marriage is a legal arrangement and so is a divorce. You already have a prenuptial agreement. It is just written by the state you got married in, if you didn't have one yourself before you got married. Thus, a separation/divorce triggers a legal process that you must familiarize yourself with if you haven't already. If you already have solid legal representation you are comfortable with, this chapter might not apply to you, but please read on if you don't. Unless you were married for a short time, have always had separate finances, do not have kids, and really only need to worry about dividing up kitchen appliances, you likely need good legal representation. You at least need to know your options, and there is probably a lot you don't know about the process. So, I encourage you to look around and consult with a lawyer about what to expect. Some will offer a free consultation, but even if not, it's worth the fee to know what you are looking at and find someone who you trust and who is negotiation-minded. It is worth booking an hour of time beyond the consultation to have all your questions answered by someone you trust. Some people have trouble deferring to experts/outsourcing, and I encourage you to consider if you fall in that category. A lot of people think they can draw up contracts on their own and just file with the court, but honestly, you will ultimately likely save time and probably a lot of arguments if you go straight to mediation or a lawyer, which are different processes. Here I outline some helpful terms and different processes of divorce (with the major caveat that I am not a lawyer and this is not legal advice!) for you to keep in mind:

COLLABORATIVE DIVORCE

A "collaborative divorce" is essentially a legal process that allows the couple to negotiate the terms of the divorce, often with the help of a mediator or legal representation for each person. The couple decides on the major issues together (i.e. marital assets, spousal support, child support, physical and legal custody). If you don't anticipate major disagreements, find a lawyer who is familiar with collaborative divorce and is negotiation-minded. They can help you get familiar with the process and answer any questions.

CONTESTED DIVORCE

A contested divorce is when the parties can't agree on major issues, and they end up in court having a judge decide for them. This is not only financially costly, but emotionally as well. I strongly encourage you to attempt to reach agreements for an uncontested divorce. A contested divorce is the hardest on kids (if they are involved) because it involves so much parental stress. I discuss a bit more on this in a later chapter on co-parenting, but for now, consider the notion that a stressful environment is the worst thing for the kids. You might think that whatever issue you are contesting is worthwhile, but I encourage you to think deeply about it. Perhaps discuss with a therapist in addition to a lawyer, because a therapist has a different lens. They might be able to help you figure out exactly why something seems important, and if it really is more important than stress in the home. The school your kids end up at might truly matter less than a stressful home environment, which is inevitable if you are involved in litigation. Of course, if it is a matter of your child's health and welfare, that is a different story. But I will say, from a therapist perspective, a lot of parents consider something to be in that category when in fact it is not. We have today's overparenting culture to thank for that, meaning that in today's parenting culture, we think every decision about our kids matters hugely and everything revolves around the kids. In the book *The Unexpected Legacy of Divorce* by Judith Wallerstein, Julia Lewis, and Sandra Blakeslee, they follow kids of divorce 25 years into adulthood. They essentially conclude that it is the conflict surrounding divorce—not the divorce itself—that is harmful for kids. Of course, most couples who get divorced have conflict. Obviously. But the takeaway is to minimize this as much as possible, and resolving issues uncontested is a major way to do that. You are helping your kids so much by minimizing conflict. So think about this when you think about issues that might go to court. When it comes to finances, I also encourage you to think about what is worth "fighting" for. Of course speak to a competent lawyer, but ultimately it is your decision. The best thing for everyone's mental health is to heal and move on, which obviously you can't do if you are entangled in a legal battle. Luckily, only about 20% of divorces are contested.

MEDIATION

Mediation is a process that involves meeting with a third party, who essentially helps the couple make their own agreement. A mediator is a go-between for each party. This process can be done all in one room, or where the mediator speaks with one party about a topic (physical custody arrangement, for example), and then conveys that preference to the other spouse, and goes back and forth ("shuttle mediation"). This is a good option for low-conflict couples, where there is amicability and most things are agreed on. It might not work for spouses with high conflict, domestic violence/emotional abuse, someone who is hiding assets, if someone has a serious untreated addiction, or if there is just an extreme level of disagreement or emotional volatility. If both parties are reasonable, this is a good option. The mediation process will result in a drafted Marital Separation Agreement (MSA), which will then be filed with the court with the final divorce decree. A major advantage to this approach is it allows for the divorce to be uncontested when it goes to the judge to grant the divorce. The other advantage is you save on lawyer fees by not having to communicate with lawyers about everything. Mediator fees are generally lower and it is more efficient.

You can also have your own legal representation in addition to mediation. This means that each individual party has someone to advise them personally while they are going through the mediation process. Your personal representation is someone in your corner, who you can ask questions and will help ultimately file and represent you at your divorce hearing (uncontested divorce or not, you will have a hearing). A good lawyer is worth the money, so invest in someone you trust. You might have to cut back on some other expenses or borrow from someone. You want to make sure you don't have to revisit issues later— at least to the extent possible, things inevitably change over-time—and an experienced lawyer will ensure that.

TL;DR

- You are already involved in a legal process, so you must be familiar with it.

- There are two different types of divorce—contested and uncontested. Shoot for the latter.

- Think VERY critically about what is worth fighting for. Possibly discuss with a therapist. More to come on this.

- Mediation is a good way to go if you are a low-conflict couple and agree on most things.

- Even if you do mediation, you probably want good individual legal representation.

- Solid, trustworthy legal representation is worth the investment. If you are resourceful, you can figure out a way to make this work.

HOMEWORK

- [ ] Do some lawyer shopping! Ask around for recommendations. Book some consults. Make sure it's a fit.

CHAPTER 3

OKAY, LET'S TALK THERAPY

How to Find the Right Help for You

*"I don't need professional help. I've
got you guys."* —CARRIE

*[Looks at watch] "For about another
ten minutes."* —SAMANTHA

"Then we're cutting you off, cold turkey." —MIRANDA

*"Hey, I don't need therapy. I need
new friends."* —CARRIE

*"Look, we're as fucked up as you are. It's like
the blind leading the blind."* —SAMANTHA

I n this scene, Carrie is obsessing about "Mr. Big" (aka Big, Carrie's love interest and an integral part of the storyline throughout the series) and her friends are cutting her off. She does ultimately go to therapy, but she stops seeing her therapist after she sleeps with the cute guy in the waiting room (Jon Bon Jovi). During their pillow talk, she asks why he's in therapy, and he tells her he completely loses interest in women immediately after he sleeps with them. She then has an epiphany that she picks the wrong men. Ah, the magic of therapy. Kidding, actually. Therapy is definitely not magic. You have to be introspective and open-minded enough to consider things from a different perspective and look at your own contribution to things. And, have actual life experiences (in this case, sex with Jon Bon Jovi) to learn from. In this chapter, I'll discuss some things to consider if you are looking for a therapist.

It might be time to look for a skilled therapist, if you don't already have one. If you do have one and you don't feel like you are getting much out of it, you could revisit your goals, or it might be time to consider a switch. There are so many reasons why this is an excellent time to find a therapist, and not just because it's in vogue these days. A marriage does not end overnight, and there is never one thing that happens to end it. More on this in a few chapters. I also firmly believe everything is a two-way street, and one person is never solely to blame for the breakdown of a marriage (there are some extreme exceptions here, including abuse, addiction, some personality disorders, but either way, even if this is the case with your spouse, you probably want to understand why you were drawn to that type of person and stayed with them). Which brings me to the first reason to find a therapist: You probably want to understand why you married someone who was ultimately not right for you. This will likely involve discussing your family of origin, where all our patterns originate! The type of environment you grew up in, your model of relationships, siblings, etc., all set the stage for later relationships. Digging into this with someone you trust can be transformative.

BARRIERS TO THERAPY

A lot of people cite financial and logistical barriers to therapy. There are affordable options for therapy including university training clinics, practices with sliding scale fees and going through your insurance (and getting a superbill if the provider is out-of-network). Think about the cost as an investment in yourself, and cut back on other things if need be, like you might do if you were to get a personal trainer (or a lawyer, as the case may be). Effective therapy can be truly transformative and is worth every penny. Telehealth makes therapy super convenient, as you can literally do it from your office or car or closet. You might be worried it'll "bring up a lot." Yes, it should! You can't fully heal with a Band Aid, sometimes you need surgery. However, it should not be only arduous without any levity, positivity, or optimism during and after sessions.

WHERE TO START

Now, I will say that going to therapy is not a no-brainer. I'm saying this as a therapist myself! It's actually not for everyone, but more importantly, the therapeutic alliance (therapist and client fit) matters much more than just "I'm in therapy, yay!" Therapy does not equal good therapy. If you don't know where to start, you can check with your insurance to find in-network providers. Most therapists have profiles on the Psychology Today website, and you can search by location, insurance, and keywords to find someone who specializes in what you are coming in with. Search "divorce," "separation," "marriage," "my wife left me I want to kill myself" (jk on that, mostly). Or whatever else you are struggling with ("anxiety," "depression," "alcohol use," "pornography use," etc.). Most therapists will offer a free consultation, though I will say that it's tough to gauge what therapy will be like with them until you actually get started. A consultation is essentially an interview, which is not therapy. So, if you find someone who seems like a good fit, there is an argument to just dive in. You'll know in a few sessions if it is someone you can see yourself trusting and opening up to.

WHAT TO LOOK FOR IN A THERAPIST

What else should you look for in a therapist? There are pros and cons of matching things like demographics and life stage. You might be more comfortable opening up to a man, or you might find that a female therapist will put you more at ease. There are significantly more female therapists, so you might have a harder time finding a male therapist who is available. I work with many men who are in difficult marriages or are divorced, and I definitely offer a perspective that is hard for them to see, which is an argument for a female therapist. It can be very helpful to talk to someone who can empathize with your spouse, in service of you understanding what went wrong. Your wife likely mentioned some things she wanted to change, and the truth is, and I say this with a warm and loving tone... where there's smoke, there's fire. There was likely a lot of truth to her words. A good therapist (regardless of demographic) can help you explore some of the things she might have said in a safe way.

Regarding other demographics, there are pros and cons of working with someone around your age: someone in your life stage might be more relatable and understand struggles they might also be dealing with, but if you identify with a therapist too much, that can also have its downsides. This is also true with race, ethnicity, religion, sexual orientation, marital status, etc. It comes down to individual preference: Only you can decide what a good fit is, but I implore you not to waste time with a therapist with whom you do not vibe, and you can't see yourself opening up to.

It is also pretty important to find a therapist that is active and engaged. There are many different therapeutic techniques/approaches. I give a brief overview of the common approaches in the next chapter, but I will say that if you find yourself with a therapist that doesn't interject much, doesn't ask though-provoking questions, doesn't give you new ways of thinking about things, and doesn't challenge you in a kind way, you might be spinning your wheels. You won't make progress with someone who just validates you, though that is important. You can spend years (and a whole lot of money) on a therapist that you like, but not make progress. If you find every session turning into a "yeah, your wife sucked" venting session, this is not actually helpful for change. You have friends or family for that, but your therapist should be someone who pushes you to examine your contribution to a dysfunctional dynamic. Nothing will change moving forward if you do not change your own behavior. I've realized I had to check myself on more than one occasion when some takeaways of my clients are "so, you're saying my wife should give me more blowjobs??" Um yes, I have said that, but the context here hugely matters, and I am also asking what THEY (my clients) are actively doing to work on their marriages. I digress, but yes, helpful therapy is not unequivocally siding with the ex.

DIAGNOSES

The Diagnostic and Statistical Manual of Mental Disorders, Fifth Edition (DSM-5), written by the American Psychological Association based on evolving research, is essentially the mental health bible. It is a reference book on mental health conditions and associated symptoms, and is one tool that therapists and psychiatrists sometimes use to try to conceptualize their clients and figure out the most effective treatment. In my opinion, despite some limitations, it is a very useful framework. If you would like to be evaluated for Depression, Anxiety, ADHD, PTSD, Substance Use Disorders, and so on, please discuss it with a mental health professional. If anyone in your life has suggested you might have any of these issues, especially your wife, introspect on this. You can also look at it yourself and see if the diagnostic criteria fit with any symptoms you may be experiencing. You know your own symptoms/experiences. Some clients find this very validating. I've gotten several referrals from people who have found their way to the DSM-5 criteria for Substance Use Disorders, or ADHD, for example, and wanted to talk to a therapist about it. I see a wide range of clinical issues in my practice, but many people during/after divorce meet criteria for what is called Adjustment Disorder. This basically means an increase in emotional and psychological symptoms following a major life stressor. So, yes! This is a thing. If you are experiencing this, you are not alone.

MEDICATION

Although I am not a prescribing doctor, I must discuss the IDEA of medication. Obviously, consult your physician or psychiatrist about this, but I just want to say a few words. Many of my clients are very resistant to the idea of psychotropic meds. Some of the reasons include: They are worried about side-effects, stigma, being on it forever, something being "wrong" with them, "needing" it, etc. I understand these concerns, AND I've seen client's mental health improve drastically with the right medication. Listen, mental health issues have biological bases. We have tons of evidence for this. Medication can help. You wouldn't refuse Insulin if you had Diabetes, or not take medication for high blood pressure. It doesn't mean there is something wrong with you; it means you could benefit from some help. Life is hard enough, especially now, why not try something that MIGHT (no guarantees) make it easier? No one should have to live with severe anxiety, depression, ADHD, etc., without the impacts being mitigated. Also, you can't claim to try everything to improve your life if you are closed-minded to medication. Again, talk to your therapist and/or prescribing doctor about the specifics, side effects, etc., but don't close the door on something that could help.

In sum, finding a good therapist CAN be transformative, but you also must be open-minded to the process and introspective. Therapists are not magicians; we can only work with what you bring us. That said, in my personal experience, when a client is willing and eager to change, it can really be life-changing. It often takes a major change like divorce to spark this. That's okay. Here you are.

COACHING

Coaching is an increasingly valuable resource as well. It is gaining legitimacy and could be quite useful. A coach could work with you on very specific issues (i.e. co-parenting, dating). This is a very different approach than therapy, as it places more emphasis on there here-and-now and less on the past/family of origin, and could be another potential useful tool.

TL;DR

- Consider looking for a therapist if you don't already have a good one.
- Therapy is accessible!
- Psychologytoday.com is a great place to start.
- Therapist/client fit is the most important predictor of success.
- A good therapist will challenge you in a warm and empathetic way.
- You can read about the diagnostic criteria for mental health disorders yourself in the DSM-5.
- Be open-minded to the idea of medication, it might help!
- Coaching might be a good option as well.

HOMEWORK

- ☐ Look at some profiles and make some calls!
- ☐ Check out the DSM-5, if you are interested in learning more about specific conditions that might be relevant to you.

CHAPTER 4

THERAPY 101

What It Is and Why It Matters

*"How can you not have a shrink! This is
Manhattan. Even the shrinks have shrinks.
I have three."* —STANFORD BLATCH

"No, you don't." —CARRIE

*"Yes, one for when I want to be coddled, one
for when I want tough love, and one for when I
want to look at a beautiful man."* —STANFORD

"That's sick!" —CARRIE

"Which is why I see the other two." —STANFORD

This quote doesn't need much explanation! Read on!

In this chapter, I'm going to give a brief overview of the types
of therapy you might encounter, so you can get a sense of what
might work for you. This might be a bit dry, but I do want you
to familiarize yourself with what is available. This isn't exhaustive, but a good start. If you look on the Psychology Today
website, you will see a lot of different approaches and you can
search by approach as well.

TYPES OF THERAPY

Cognitive Behavioral Therapy (CBT)

Cognitive-Behavioral Therapy (CBT) is fairly ubiquitous these days, and is the gold-standard for many types of anxiety and depression. CBT involves looking at the relationship between your thoughts (cognitions), feelings, and behaviors. Imagine a triangle connecting all three of those things, because they all influence each other. There are hundreds of textbooks and manuals written on CBT (refer to the recommended readings for examples). CBT is considered an evidence-based treatment for anxiety, depression, substance-use, and many other mental health disorders. Here, I'm just going to give one example of a CBT technique:

Let's say you have the thought, *"I can never do anything to make my wife happy."* What might you *feel* as a result? Likely pretty sad, hopeless, anxious, angry, frustrated. And what might these feelings lead you to *do* (behaviors)? Perhaps disengage or withdraw from her, maybe drink, shutdown, etc. As a consequence of those behaviors, you might feel even MORE down on yourself, and have even more self-destructive thoughts. See how these all interconnect?

A cognitive-behavioral approach will help you identify and challenge these maladaptive (i.e. harmful) thoughts into more accurate and helpful ones. So, in the example above, here are a few ways to reframe (attention: important therapy word there) that unhelpful thought above:

"Things have been tough lately and my wife seems unhappy. I wonder what I can do to help understand her more."

"My wife seems unhappy, and I likely have something to do with it. I have influence over how she feels in both positive and negative ways."

"I love my wife and I want to help her. I want to understand my role in her unhappiness."

If you had any of the above thoughts, how might that change your feelings and your behavior? You might feel more hopeful, optimistic, connected, etc. Different behaviors will occur as a result (i.e. approach instead of withdraw). You might do something she has been asking you to do, give her some words of affirmation, or a loving hug. As a result, you might feel more confident, connected, and close and want to continue these behaviors.

As stated above, the CBT triangle connects in all different directions. A CBT-oriented therapist can be more cognitively focused, which means helping to identify your unhelpful thought patterns and challenge these thoughts, with the goal of you learning to challenge them yourself. The ultimate goal here is to increase cognitive flexibility by helping you identify and ultimately change global, negative, and rigid thought patterns. They might take a more behavioral approach (more on this below), which is focusing more on what you are *doing*, with the goal of changing your thinking patterns and feelings as a result of changing behaviors. You can never just change your emotions. They are not a light switch; you can't just "feel better." You have to first identify and then change the thing that leads to that emotion, which, according to CBT, is a thought or behavior.

Behavioral Therapy / Behavioral Activation

This approach targets… you guessed it, behaviors! Behavioral therapy encourages people to think in general about their values, or what is important to them in life. When people are living a life in accordance with their values, this is a huge buffer against anxiety and depression. The reverse is also true. When people's values are incongruous with their behaviors, depression and anxiety can skyrocket. You likely saw this in your marriage. For example, if you value a loving partnership but that doesn't exist for you and you aren't actively working toward it, your behaviors are not in line with your values, and this can be quite depressing. Another example: If you value a healthy lifestyle but you aren't exercising, this can cause guilt and shame because your actions are not aligning with your values of having a healthy lifestyle.

A value is like a compass. It is something you are always working toward, rather than a line item to "check off". For example, a value of mine is to be successful in my business. There is no way I can check that off as a completed value and say, *"I achieved it. I reached the 'business success' value,"* but rather it is a guide, because I can always continue to move in that direction. So I can have *goals* in line with that value. For example, writing this book or getting X number of new clients or posting daily on Instagram. Those I can "check off." A behavioral therapist might have you identify your values and the concrete steps you can take to work toward them, and help you break down those steps into measurable and accomplishable tasks. An effective behavioral technique is breaking things down into SMART goals (specific, measurable, achievable, realistic, and timely). It can be very overwhelming and sometimes paralyzing to think about your goals, especially doing this period of your life. You might be thinking, *"I have to set up an entire house,"* or *"I have to get back in shape.*" A behavioral therapist will help you break down this large goal into smaller, doable steps. As you accomplish each of these smaller goals (i.e. picking out a shower curtain, getting a gym membership), you will feel proud, accomplished, and motivated to continue. Behavioral therapy addresses thoughts and feelings through *changing behavior*, and working toward living a life in line with your values!

Acceptance and Commitment Therapy (ACT)

ACT is also a very effective treatment for anxiety, depression, and substance use. ACT is centered around values as well, but is quite different from CBT in that this approach emphasizes *accepting* your negative thoughts and emotions, and not allowing them to get in the way of your behavior. ACT focuses a ton on mindfulness for the acceptance piece and identifying and working toward your values for the commitment piece. It's approach is basically, *"fuck those thoughts and feelings telling you that you can't do something. You aren't going to change them, and you can spend your energy trying to change them, or you can focus on doing the things that are important to you anyway, and take that negative thought/ feeling right along with you."*

An example of this would be, you have the thought *"this girl is way too hot for me, and she will never date me."* You might feel hopeless and sad as a result. In CBT, you might challenge this thought with something like *"I've dated attractive women before and it's been fine! There is no such thing as 'out of my league', I got this!"* with the idea that this reframe would change the feeling and result in different behavior. An ACT perspective would say that "fighting" your thoughts/feelings like that is not actually effective; that you don't really buy the new thought, and therefore, it wouldn't change your behavior. So instead, ACT would teach you mindfulness techniques and use metaphors to help you *accept* that you are going to have these thoughts, and will ask you what the *value* is behind pursuing the girl you are interested in, and encourage you to connect with that value. If you have a strong connection with your values and move in the direction of a valued life, those negative thoughts/emotions might still be there, but they won't get in the way of living your best (valued!) life.

Dialectical Behavior Therapy (DBT)

DBT was originally developed for people with Borderline Personality Disorder (BPD), and is, in its full form, a fairly intensive treatment that targets extreme impulsivity, emotion dysregulation, substance use, suicidal behaviors, self-injury, along with more common issues like depression and anxiety. It consists of skill building in the form of a class, plus individual therapy, and as-needed phone coaching. Few programs offer "full model" DBT, but many therapists are "DBT-informed," like myself. I was part of the DBT team at the group practice before I started my own practice, and I use a lot of the principles in my work. Although it was developed for more severe populations, DBT is useful for almost every human on the planet because it teaches emotion regulation, distress tolerance, mindfulness, and interpersonal effectiveness. If you struggle with any of the issues I mentioned before, you might want to look into full model DBT, but otherwise a therapist who is knowledgeable about DBT can be a good fit. It essentially has a lot of elements of CBT and ACT, with an emphasis on mindfulness. The tools used for DBT are largely behavioral, with lots of emphasis on values.

Trauma treatment and exposure therapy for anxiety

I am lumping these together because most intensive trauma treatments involve some form of exposure therapy, though exposure therapy can also be very effective for non-trauma related anxiety. There are various types of trauma treatment (Prolonged Exposure Therapy, Cognitive Processing Therapy, EMDR, to name a few). Through various techniques, these all involve essentially exposing yourself to memories of a traumatic event or events in a structured and systematic way (that varies depending on the approach) in order to understand the events, and eventually reach a place of acceptance of the past (complete with all the emotions surrounding it). The "exposure" piece is exposing yourself to the anxiety that comes along with recounting memories of these events. Many of the above treatments also involve real-life exposure therapy, meaning actively engaging (also in a systematic way) in the things that you might be avoiding due to trauma and anxiety (some examples below). The urge with anxiety and trauma is to avoid painful memories, activities, and associated feelings. Trauma therapy encourages you to approach instead. It is kind of like surgery. If you don't really dig in, you can't get to the root of the issue and ultimately heal from it. There is often a lot of trauma at the root of dysfunctional relationships, and sometimes people can't move forward unless this trauma is addressed. So, this is something to consider when thinking about your mental health following divorce.

When I worked at veteran hospitals, I was constantly amazed by the dedication and resilience of my clients. Many of them had been through unimaginable trauma, and did NOT want to talk about it, let alone recount the incidents in the level of detail that some of these treatments require. Once these clients decided to give it a go, it was incredible. One client comes to mind.

He was an impeccably dressed physician (had been a medic in the military). Looking at him, you would never know what he was dealing with. The nightmares, the intrusive thoughts, the shame and guilt. His PTSD, expectedly, had a huge impact on his marriage and he was on the brink of divorce. He was committed to doing the work because he couldn't commit to something and not follow through (sometimes the rigid thinking works in the therapist's favor!). He couldn't send an email without checking it a hundred times to make sure it was perfect. We discussed how examples like these were a way of compensating and controlling things, when he had been so out of control of what had happened to him during his service. He cried in my office as he relived the memory we were working on over and over. Then, he would roll up his perfect sleeves and go to work and home to his wife. With time and intensive trauma therapy, his rigidity decreased, he was able to release some self-hatred and blame, and spent way less time on emails. I couldn't quite convince him to dress less perfect... you win some, you lose some. Anyway, if you are experiencing what you think might be trauma-related symptoms, I encourage you to look for a trauma-focused therapist. A good therapist will be "trauma-informed" anyway, which means they will look at your presenting issues with an eye on past traumas and approach it from that lens. However, if you want more structured trauma treatment, look for the approaches I mentioned above.

Exposure therapy is also very effective for specific phobias (for example, fear of heights, water, etc.), panic disorder (panic attacks), social anxiety, and OCD. The idea is that you expose yourself in a systematic way to the feared stimulus, and you sit with the feelings of anxiety and fear that come up, rather than using your typical coping mechanisms (likely avoidance) to make the anxiety go away. Avoidance ultimately doesn't work. So, for example, if you are afraid of heights or crowds or social rejection, you and your therapist would figure out ways to get yourself exposed to these situations, and you would learn many things from this! You would learn: the thing you are worried about happening (i.e. falling off a bridge you are scared to cross, being entirely socially rejected), likely will not happen. If it does happen, you will learn that you can live with it and it is not the end of the world. You will also learn that your anxiety will go away; it won't kill you. And you will learn that you can do the thing you are afraid of! It's incredible to see the confidence that comes with this kind of work. I would say I incorporate some form of exposure therapy in most of my work, even if it's not in a super systematic way. Regarding trauma treatment, the exposure is focused specifically on the trauma and the things you avoid as a result. This can be truly transformative.

As this relates to divorce, you are probably shying away from a lot of trauma in your marriage and probably honestly in your upbringing. I have some questions/food for thought on your childhood below, but as a general statement: people don't usually stay in dysfunctional relationships if they had examples of functional relationships growing up. The relationships that you saw are blueprints for romantic relationships. You are drawn to specific people for a reason, that often reflects a dysfunctional childhood and poor models of a marriage. If you think this might ring true for you, it is definitely worth discussing in therapy. Also, divorce in itself is essentially a huge exposure exercise. You are essentially forced into a situation where you have no control and you have to deal with the feelings! Especially if you did not initiate the divorce. Parenting is also good practice for this. For many of my clients, divorce did wonders for their anxiety because they cannot control what happens when their kids are with their co-parent. This is actually a good thing! As long as the kids are safe, most things don't actually matter to the degree you think they do.

Psychodynamic/psychoanalytic

Psychodynamic therapy is focused on exploring the unconscious motivations for behavior, which are often rooted in the past. Think Freud on this one. From this perspective, the key to understanding current problems/behaviors is to unlock the unconscious, which holds a ton of stuff from the past. This is a very non-directive approach, guided by the client. In this approach, the therapist may take the client's lead and not push them in any one direction, though this does vary by therapist. This approach involves a lot of discussion of the past, including past traumas. There are different types of approaches under the umbrella of psychodynamic therapy, with the therapist being more or less active depending on their individual style.

Couple's therapy

I won't spend too much time here because this book is intended to be helpful for your individual journey, but there are several different modalities of couples therapy (some of which you may have tried with your ex). Emotion-focused Couples Therapy, Integrative Behavioral Couple's Therapy, Imago therapy, The Gottman Method (this is more of an approach), and more. A good couple's therapist will also talk about sex and make it a focus (this is true regardless of couple's or individual therapy). A good thing to think about moving forward if you have a new partner, is when to know if couple's therapy would be helpful. So many couples I see come in crisis, and they are far beyond "fixing." I wish many of them had come sooner. I also practice what is called "discernment counseling," which means that I help couples decide for themselves if they are a good fit for each other and if the relationship is really what they want.

There are a few other modalities that I did not mention that are beyond the scope of this book, but those are the general approaches. Feel free to ask potential therapists what their approach is! Remember, the client/therapist FIT is more important than the actual approach, so make sure that it feels right. The unhelpful kind of therapy is the kind where the therapist says nothing for the entire session, nods in support of whatever you say, and takes your money. Not an effective approach.

GAUGING PROGRESS

How do you know when you are making progress with a therapist? You'll know when you are making progress when you are entertaining different ways of thinking about things, gaining new insights about your patterns, learning to identify and sit with uncomfortable/tough emotions, and ultimately actually changing behavior. Additionally, though a present-focused approach is important, you also won't make real progress if you don't understand where some of your patterns likely originate. A good therapist must ask about your family of origin and help you draw some connections there.

Here are some questions that a skilled therapist should be asking you (some regarding family of origin, some not. This list is not exhaustive, but a good start. Also these are just good questions for you to think about on your own!):

- What was your family landscape?

- Are there mental health issues in your family (depression, anxiety, addiction, trauma)?

- Where are you in the birth order (if you have siblings)?

- What was your sibling dynamic? Was there a favorite?

- Were you able to go to a caregiver for emotional support?

- How did your parents handle your emotions?

- Did your parents share their emotions with each other?

- Did your parents have fun with each other?

- What did you learn about adulthood? Was it all bills and chores, or was there also fun and excitement (the latter is so important to model!)?

- How did you spend your weekends? This is relevant for the above question; if weekends are all chores and no fun, you grow up thinking adulthood is just a slog.

- How would you characterize your parents' marriage?

- Did you have one parent that assumed a "caretaker" role for the other?

- How did your parents resolve conflict (if they did)?

- What did you learn about gender roles?

- Did your parents take each other's side when it came to the kids in your household?

- Did your parents undermine each other's parenting?

- Were your parents critical of you?

- Did you witness any (or all) of the following behaviors among your parents: criticism, contempt, stonewalling, defensiveness (these are the four horsemen of the apocalypse and will be explained in depth in the next chapter)?

- Did your parents give you honest feedback about your strengths and challenges, or did they just praise you regardless of your efforts?

- Did your parents share stories about their own childhood?

- Did you feel like you had to take care of one or both parents?

- Did your parents criticize each other to you?

- Did they say positive things about each other to you?

- Were your parents physically attracted to each other? How could you tell?

- Did your parents flirt with each other? Touch each other?

- Were your parents romantic toward each other?

- What was the gift giving culture in your household?

- What did you learn about physical touch in romantic relationships?

- What did you learn about sex?

- What was the attitude like in your house in general (was it open-minded and optimistic, or negative and rigid)?

- Did your parents encourage a culture of trying new things, saying yes to things, etc.?

- Were your parents judgmental of each other? What about other people?

- Did your parents give compliments to each other?

- Did they talk each other up in front of you?

- Did they make each other laugh?

- What did their other relationships look like (with friends, family, colleagues)?

- Did your parents respect each other's professional goals and hobbies? Did they roll their eyes or make fun of each other's jobs or how they spent their time otherwise? Or did they support and cheerlead each other?

This list is obviously not exhaustive! But it should get you thinking. You'll notice that most of the questions above are about how your parents might have treated each other, not necessarily how they treated you. This is because the latter is important, but the former is really the blueprint for what we learn about romantic relationships. Though, of course, how you were parented also matters. I often recommend the book *Adult Children of Emotionally Immature Parents: How to Heal From Distant, Rejecting, or Self-Involved Parents* by Lindsay Gibson to my clients in order to introspect about their upbringing. Think about some of these questions and the models you had for marriage. Start to consider that you may have been drawn to someone who shared some of the qualities of your caregivers, for subconscious reasons. This is not pop psychology bullshit. You can read more about this in the book *Getting the Love you Want* by Harville Hendrix. I touch on this a bit later as well. The above are all important questions for introspection and/or therapy, and a good therapist will help you explore them in a safe space.

Again, though this book is not a substitute for therapy, and even if you don't find a therapist right now, think about some of these questions! We all learn from somewhere, and I am consistently surprised by how many clients of mine have never thought about any of these questions. A good therapist will also explore attachment styles, which also is now somehow a universal conversation, even to the point of being on dating profiles. I am going to provide an overview of attachment styles in a later chapter.

TL;DR:

- There are many different modalities of therapy.
- Some modalities like CBT, BA, DBT, ACT, and some types of exposure therapy focus on the here-and-now, while others like trauma-focused therapy and psychodynamic approaches focus on the past and the unconscious motivations for behaviors.
- Understanding your family of origin is crucial to self-growth and development.
- We all have a relationship blueprint we get from our family.
- Therapists should be asking about family of origin and learned patterns.

HOMEWORK

- ☐ Introspect on the list above regarding family of origin and parental dynamics.
- ☐ Answer 5 of the above questions (either as a thought exercise or write them down!).

CHAPTER 5

WHAT JUST HAPPENED?!

A Straightforward Look at Why Marriages Fall Apart

"I don't know how you survived any of it, Big or Aidan. This love stuff is a motherfucker." —SAMANTHA

"Love? Did you just say 'love?'" —CHARLOTTE

"Oh, what the hell! My name is Samantha and I'm a loveaholic." —SAMANTHA

"Hi, Samantha!" —CHORUS OF ALL THREE OF THEM

"It's so infuriating! I mean, where can this possibly go? No one actually makes these relationship things work, do they?" —SAMANTHA

In this scene, Samantha is confessing to the girls that she is in love with Richard (who was mentioned in the "feelings" chapter opening). Samantha, who had avoided love like the plague until that point, felt like a fish out of water. She is obviously skeptical that "these relationship things" can work. Sadly, it takes a whole lot more than love to make a relationship work. In this chapter, I will highlight the things I've seen in my practice that contribute to the dissolution of a marriage. These are of course general patterns, so they might not apply, but hopefully will give you some things to think about. It is difficult to look back and think about what went wrong, and your contribution, but it is critical if you want to understand your past relationships, heal, and move forward with important lessons.

LOOKING BACK- BLOWJOBS AND LOVE LETTERS

In addition to feeling pretty intense feelings right now, you might be trying to figure out what happened/what went wrong in your marriage. As I said before, this book is not a substitute for therapy, but I do want to share what I often see from a general standpoint regarding what leads to things falling apart. Often, people are not compatible to begin with and ignore a lot of red flags. I will also discuss more on compatibility later on. People often think there is some big drama that leads to divorce: affairs, secrets, financial betrayals, or addictions. While that does happen some of the time, it is not the norm. And, when they do happen, it is often the result of many years of disconnection, for example in the case of affairs. More often, however, it is "just" the withering away of the love and commitment to make the other person feel like a priority. The little ruptures. The disengagement that happens every day. Brushing things under the rug. The marriage itself moving farther and farther down the totem pole of priorities. A missed compliment. A sexual rejection. A forgotten anniversary. Resentment building over all these things. Each incident itself isn't "worth" saying something (a myth!). When this happens hundreds or thousands of times, each person starts to feel incredibly lonely and unloved.

My favorite analogy for this is love letters and blowjobs. This is not an uncommon analogy. There is a great podcast by a famous divorce lawyer (who endorsed this book!), James Sexton (@nycdivorcelawyer on Instagram), where he uses blowjobs and granola as the analogy, and a great psychologist, Dr. Samantha Rodman-Whiten (@drpsychmom on Instagram), who uses blowjobs and flowers, but I like blowjobs and love letters. It's all to highlight the same ideas.

Let's take a fictional couple, Liz and Tom. Liz loves receiving love notes/letters (she's a words of affirmation girl), and Tom loves blowjobs (physical touch is his love language). Hard to imagine, I know (I know this analogy is stereotypical, but this is often what I see in my practice!). When Tom and Liz are both receiving love letters and blowjobs, respectively, they are feeling very loved, attended to, cared for, and prioritized. Especially when they know the other person is going out of their way to do these things. When Liz and Tom start dating, Liz gives Tom a lot of blowjobs, and Tom makes sure to leave Liz little notes at her house, and writes longer, more detailed letters for her birthday and for their anniversaries (which he acknowledges on a monthly basis). This is all pretty easy in the beginning because of New Relationship Energy (NRE; more on that later).

Then, one day, he is in a hurry and doesn't leave a note. She decides she's too tired for a blowjob. She instead has penetrative sex with Tom, which she considers to be more efficient, or doesn't engage in sexual activity at all. Liz and Tom are kind and understanding people, so they don't get mad at each other. They might be a little disappointed, but no worries. They don't say anything.

This happens again. Neither say anything again. It happens several more times. Soon, it has been years since both of these things occurred, and they are both feeling disconnected and unloved, because they are not receiving the things that make them feel loved. I have a whole chapter on love languages later in the book.

When people aren't receiving love in the way that makes them feel loved, they feel hurt, rejected, isolated, and unimportant. After a long time of this, it is hard to come back from. As people go through life, which gets harder and harder, and requires more of a strong partnership, it becomes even more important, and people feel even worse when it doesn't happen.

A marriage does not end because of one put off blowjob, one dropped ball on an anniversary, one pile of dishes in the sink. You can read Matthew Fray's *Huffington Post* essay, "She Divorced Me Because I left Dishes By The Sink." It is not one time, it's years of accumulation of these things, where both partners feel more and more disconnected and less and less seen and understood. It takes both people to contribute to this dynamic, and it doesn't happen overnight. Once you get far apart, it takes a whole lot of work to come back. It is possible, and I have certainly seen it in my practice. Both partners have to love (and like!) each other, be committed to the marriage, be open-minded to going out of their comfort zone and trying things differently, be willing to accept responsibility for their part in the deterioration of things and past ruptures (this piece is HUGE), and be willing to introspect on the root causes (which is often related to family of origin). These are all things we work on in couple's therapy. However, by the time they come to me, it is often too late. It is tough to get accurate data on the success of couple's therapy, because it depends on how "success" is defined, but evidence suggests that couple's therapy can be helpful for about 70% of couples. Most say that therapy leads to a greater understanding, better communication, and more intimacy. However, many couples wait too long to come to therapy. By the time they get to me, there is too much distance, hurt, resentment, blame, anger, and contempt.

SCOREKEEPING

Scorekeeping is unfortunately incredibly common in relationships and very toxic. This is the practice of keeping track of everything you consider yourself to be doing in/for the relationship and the other person. When couples get into a pattern of this, it is very difficult to get out of. From what I see in my practice, neither person recognizes the other's contribution to the relationship/household. This sounds a lot like:

Partner 1: *"I made dinner, folded the laundry, helped the kids with their homework, booked our flights for the holidays. What did you do??"*

Partner 2: *"I was working! I wasn't just out with my friends messing around. I have to work! And by the way, I cleaned the house and paid the bills and chauffeured the kids all around today."*

And so on. These conversations, of course, go nowhere, because neither person is actually listening to the other, and they are just getting defensive (more on that in a minute). There is also very often a lack of appreciation for the things the other person does. The thing that a lot of couples don't realize is many people do things for the household and the kids, but they stop doing things for EACH OTHER, like I talked about above (blowjobs and love letters). It is hard to appreciate the things that someone would be doing anyway, for themselves or the kids for example (i.e. laundry, paying bills, driving around). The reason it is not appreciated fully is because it is not actually for your partner. Many married people only focus on the things they do for the house, the kids, extended family, etc., and not truly for each other. Ask yourself: are the things you claimed to be doing for your wife things you would be doing anyway? For example, taking the kids to school, cleaning, bills, etc.? Those don't "count", because they were not specifically for your partner. If your wife was away, or sick, or now that you are divorced or in the process of divorce, you are still doing those things. Neither partner feels loved with the things their partner would be doing anyway. You wouldn't be buying specific paper towels she liked, or again - writing love letters, if you weren't with her. THOSE are things that "count." Of course, many partners also don't, in fact, recognize and appreciate everything their partners ARE doing. This, of course, leads to a lot of resentment. In your next relationships, it is so important to recognize the other person's contributions (this is positive scorekeeping!) and also to make sure they are aware of yours! Share the things you go out of your way to do for them, in a kind and loving way. For example, "I bought your favorite ice cream tonight even though it wasn't on sale because I love you so much!" This is letting your partner know they are on your mind, in a loving way as opposed to a resentful way. This was very likely not something you did in your marriage. Anyway, these are things to think about moving forward (much more to come on this), but we will continue to look back.

THE FOUR HORSEMEN

This brings me to an important concept in couple's therapy/ research: The Four Horsemen of the Apocalypse. This "four horsemen" concept was developed by John and Julie Gottman in their research on couples, and the purpose of them is to identify the behaviors that cause the most disconnection and predict divorce. They are as follows: contempt, criticism, stonewalling, and defensiveness.

Contempt

Contempt, according to the researchers, is the single biggest predictor of divorce. I can spot contempt in .5 seconds in my sessions when I meet a couple, and the outcomes are not great. Contemptuous behaviors include: eye rolling (this one is HUGE), mocking, imitating, and other behaviors that signal intense dislike (even hatred) and disrespect for your partner. I will die on the hill that reality TV is excellent to watch with your partner (more on that later), and there are some shows where you can see the contempt these partners have for each other. It's hard to watch and hard to come back from if it is present in your relationship.

Criticism

Criticism is, of course, that. It is probably one of the most common of the four horsemen. It can be blatant insults, as in "you're lazy," "what's wrong with you??", "you're so dumb," etc. These are pretty obviously toxic. Also, if you are "joking" in this way, it is still criticism and pretty bad. However, it is not always as blatant as it might seem to be. Of course, it is direct criticism as in, "you're a bad driver" and "you're a terrible parent." However, it is also more subtle than that. Both men and women are guilty of the "subtle" criticism.

For example:

"You're packing *that* for our daughter's lunch?"

"Just let me do it, it's faster."

"Why would you load the dishwasher that way?"

"You forgot the tomatoes AGAIN?"

"You never ask me how my day was."

"Ugh, that shirt??"

"Are you going to go back to the gym soon?"

...and so on. Yes, this is criticism! It makes your partner feel like they are doing something wrong, and it signals that you don't respect their choices/ways of doing things. It is completely fine to ask for things to be done a certain way within the context of a loving, secure attachment (more on this later), but this is not that way. Criticism erodes self-esteem and confidence, and makes the partner on the receiving end feel pretty terrible and rejected. There are ways to voice your needs that are kind and loving (more on that later).

Stonewalling

Stonewalling is shutting down; basically refusing to engage in conversation. This can be evidenced by literally walking away, turning away, stopping to talk, saying the words "I'm not talking about this anymore" (or something similar), etc. This is usually a result of feeling so emotionally overwhelmed that you cannot engage. However, it is a fairly dysfunctional way of communicating this. It is effectively putting a metaphorical wall up between you and the person you are talking to. If you have been on the receiving end of this, you likely know how frustrating it is. This is the behavior that could lead to screaming and/or other aggressive behaviors because someone is so emotionally inaccessible. This also plays into attachment dynamics (see next chapter on this), as stonewalling is a definite example of avoidant attachment, and certainly drives a pursuer insane.

Defensiveness

And lastly, defensiveness. Also incredibly common, and a sneaky one! Like criticism, many people don't realize they are being defensive. Defensiveness is essentially a lack of accountability for something, and there is often an automatic "it's not my fault" response. For example, John tells Megan, "You forgot about my work happy hour tonight that I was really hoping you'd make it to." Megan responds, "Ugh, ok!!! Don't you know how busy I am?? Why are there happy hours all the time anyway?! And you should have reminded me if it was so important!!" See how this is defensive? Megan could have said, "Arg, you're right! I'm so sorry. It totally slipped my mind." In secure relationships, people don't mind being reminded (in a loving way) of things they forgot, but when things are rocky, people get very defensive. There is often a lot of resentment built up underneath the defensiveness. Taking responsibility is key and leads to less defensiveness overall.

Think back to your marriage. I would bet you had all of these, likely in spades. Think about your OWN behaviors regarding the four horsemen, as I'm sure you are already thinking about your ex's. Gotta take ownership here in order to learn and grow! Also consider, as discussed in the last chapter, if these behaviors were present in the marriage(s) you saw growing up. Remember, they are blueprints, so you likely learned this from somewhere.

APOLOGIZING/REPAIRING RUPTURES

On the topic of defensiveness, I wanted to take a minute to talk about apologizing, because this is such a huge issue I see with my clients (men and women alike). When you are looking back on your marriage, ask yourself if your ex-wife ever shared feelings of frustration over you not apologizing or taking responsibility. I see this in my practice all the time where one partner "holds on" to a past rupture, and the other partner is frustrated that they haven't "let it go." A "rupture" in this case is referring to hurting your partner. This can be a massive rupture (i.e. an affair), or a smaller one (i.e. forgetting to let your partner know you'll be home late for dinner). If it hurts your partner and there is a breach of trust (no matter how big), it is what is called an empathic rupture. Here's the thing: people only "hold onto" anger when they don't feel as though they have been truly heard and empathized with. A sincere and meaningful apology is a bit of an art. There are whole books written on apologies, as well as an "apology language" quiz online to determine how you best receive apologies! The most effective apologies are the ones that a.) acknowledge responsibility, b.) use the words "I'm sorry" (in an authentic and sincere way), c.) express an understanding of why what they did was hurtful, and d.) include a statement about change. Affirming words don't hurt either. Of course, you can't promise to never hurt someone again (we are human!), but one can promise to try and to communicate differently.

Here is an example (with helpful annotations!) of an effective apology, using the scenario that a husband forgot to make a reservation for his wife's birthday:

Husband: "I am so sorry I forgot to make a reservation for your birthday [acknowledgement, responsibility, and apology all in one!]. I know how much you wanted to go to this restaurant [empathy], and I know they require reservations well in advance [more responsibility!]. I don't want you to think your birthday isn't important to me [empathy and affirmations]. I very much want to celebrate you and all you do for our family. I love you so much and I want you to feel special [more

affirmations]. I promise we will go to this restaurant another time, and in the meantime I will find a different way to celebrate on your birthday **[actionable plan to repair]**. You are wonderful and deserve it" **[more affirmations!]**.

Ta-da! And then you actually follow up with the stated plan. Crucial detail. Often, acknowledging responsibility is the hardest part; people do not like to admit when they were wrong, or that they hurt their loved one. This is the first sentence in the above example. More often, someone will say something like, "This restaurant is impossible! It isn't my fault!" This is the opposite of taking responsibility. Admitting you messed up can often come with a lot of shame, which leads to avoidance. This is understandable! It's very hard to admit that you've hurt or disappointed someone whom you likely pride yourself on protecting. However, this is human! We all make mistakes, and we all hurt people we care about. It's about taking responsibility. Another barrier to apologizing is something like, "Well, I don't want to bring something back up. Things are okay." But guess what... often, the hurt partner is already thinking about it! It is so validating to name the "elephant in the room." Acknowledging the rupture is showing that it is on your mind as well, that you care. This does not "let people off the hook," as is a common myth for people who are rigid thinkers: that apologizing means their behavior is okay or condoned. As though an apology makes everything acceptable. On the contrary, there is a major difference between an excuse and an explanation. Making mistakes is part of being human. It can be a really beautiful thing when an apology is expressed fully and authentically, and accepted. Of course, if trust is broken, it takes time and doing things differently to rebuild. A full apology is necessary but not sufficient for repair.

I actually think the ability to effectively repair after an argument/hurt feelings is one of the most important things in a relationship. By virtue of existing in the world, we will hurt people we care about. The point is not to avoid that; the point is to repair after. When people can come together and hear each other and repair, it can be powerful and stabilizing. And if not, it can have serious long-lasting effects.

Although not entirely comprehensive or specific to your exact situation, I hope this chapter provided some helpful insight into where things might have gone south in your marriage. Throughout the book, I continue to point out additional factors that I see contribute to divorce (sex and love languages being huge ones, I have chapters on those in a bit), and there will be much more opportunities for looking back and self-reflection. This is a critical component of learning from the past and moving on.

TL;DR

- Most marriages end in death by a thousand cuts, not one big issue.
- Scorekeeping (the bad kind) is toxic and common.
- Four horsemen are good predictors of divorce.
- Apologizing is really important, and there are more and less effective ways of doing so.

HOMEWORK/QUESTIONS TO CONSIDER

☐ Introspect on the four horsemen that were present in your marriage.

☐   How did YOU exhibit some of these behaviors?

☐   How did you and your ex work through arguments? How are you with apologizing?

CHAPTER 6

AM I REALLY AVOIDANT?

The Truth About Attachment
Styles and Relationships

*"Did I ever really love Big? Or was I addicted
to the pain, the exquisite pain, of wanting
someone so unattainable?"* —CARRIE

C arrie wonders this after she and Big break up for the second time because he announces he is moving to Paris and does not "factor her in" or discuss it in any real, open way. He says he needs to be in a relationship where if he has to go to Paris, he "has to go to Paris," and tells her if she is going to go with him, she should go for her, because he does not want her to "uproot her life and expect anything." Carrie gets so upset by the realization that Big continues to pull away that she throws their McDonalds against the wall and breaks up with him. Carrie and Big's relationship exemplified the pursuer/withdrawer relationship from the beginning, and it unfolds throughout. Carrie always wanted more than Big could give her. The more vulnerable she wanted him to be, the more he pulled away. Big had an avoidant attachment style, and was threatened by vulnerability, and thus withdrew in an attempt to protect himself. Carrie had an anxious/preoccupied attachment style. She was obsessed with him from the beginning. The more he withdrew, the more she pursued, and the more she pursued, the more he withdrew. Both are likely using protective mechanisms developed in childhood (more to come on this). Carrie also obsessed over every interaction (this is not limited to Big), and instead of communicating to the person she was with, she would spiral either internally or to her girlfriends (case in point, when they told her to get a therapist, referenced in chapter three). I could actually write a lot about all the character's attachment styles, but I'll spare you (this time). In this chapter, I will discuss the origins of Attachment Theory from a developmental framework (this is how it started, after all), how they manifest in adult relationships, and how they can change.

Understanding attachment in general, and as it relates to you, is paramount to understanding relationships and your individual patterns. I will provide an overview of attachment here, but for a more in-depth discussion, I recommend reading the book *Attached* by Amir Levine and Rachel Heller. It is so important that entire approaches to therapy, such as Emotion-Focused Couple's Therapy, are based on attachment theory. For more reading on that, take a look at *Hold Me Tight: Seven Conversations for a Lifetime of Love* by Sue Johnson. Everything you hear these days about attachment all originated from a Developmental Psychologist named Mary Ainsworth. She developed the "strange situation" paradigm in the 1970s, where she and her colleagues observed babies who were left alone by their caregivers for a brief period of time. The paradigm was this: A caregiver and their baby (9-30 months old) would come into a room full of toys. At various points, the caregiver and the stranger would enter and exit the room, leaving the baby alone with either the caregiver, the stranger, both of them, or neither of them. The babies' responses to various scenarios were observed, and divided into four different attachment styles based on their reactions:

SECURE ATTACHMENT

The babies who were later categorized as securely attached played freely while their caregivers were present and also when they left. The babies engaged with the stranger while the caregiver was present, might have been upset when the caregiver left but recovered quickly, and they were happy when they returned and easily comforted. These securely attached children feel able to explore because they have a "secure base." They know they will be taken care of, and they trust that their caregiver won't leave them. A child becomes securely attached when a caregiver is responsible, reliable, predictable, loving, and able to meet their needs appropriately. As adults, securely attached individuals are comfortable leaving their partners and vise-versa, but they are also comfortable relying on each other to meet their needs, being emotionally and physically vulnerable (which goes along with relying on a partner because asking for things is vulnerable), and being themselves. They are confident in what they have to give and are confident in what they deserve. The healthiest relationships are between two securely attached individuals. Paired together, securely attached individuals can be themselves because they are accepted and loved by the person, and they don't fear judgment or abandonment. Think of a secure base like a firmly planted beach umbrella. The partner of said umbrella can take risks and go in the water, can play on the beach nearby or shop on the boardwalk, and can even drive far away because they know they will be taken care of when they return. If the umbrella is shaky, one cannot go far because they are afraid it will topple over and they won't be protected. This pairing can communicate openly and honestly, ask for what they want, receive feedback, apologize and repair effectively, have fun together and take risks, and they typically have an active and exploratory sex life.

INSECURE ATTACHMENT

The other category of babies in this paradigm were the insecurely attached ones. There are several types of insecure attachment types:

Avoidant attachment:

The avoidant attachment type babies essentially ignored their caregiver. They showed little emotion when their caregiver left or returned. They were emotionally detached, because they were not sure they could count on their caregiver to provide the secure base that they needed to explore. Essentially, the caregiver had not been consistently responsive to their attachment needs (for example, being unavailable when their baby reached out for comfort). Interestingly, the babies did not show outward distress, but later experiments using heart rate monitors confirmed the hypothesis that these babies were indeed distressed, and the detachment was a protective mechanism in order to not get too close and find their needs were unmet. These individuals will grow up to be more "independent" and withdrawn, and have a hard time relying on other people.

It is quite difficult for adults with avoidant attachment to be vulnerable in relationships; they have learned that other people will let them down (because their caregivers did), so they don't rely on others. It is incredibly difficult to have a close, emotionally (and physically) connected relationship with someone with avoidant attachment, because closeness and intimacy inherently requires vulnerability, and avoidantly-attached individuals do not do vulnerability well. It isn't their fault, but the effect on relationships is the same. These are often the people who say they don't have any needs in relationships, let alone state what they are. Sex can also be an area of vulnerability for them, so often they will focus more on their partner and not their own pleasure. Initially this can be mistaken as a positive, but the effect of it is that they don't get their needs met and the resentment builds.

Here are some clues that someone has avoidant attachment: Not revealing much about themselves, always turning the conversation to the other person and giving lots of attention in order to take the heat off them, possibly a reluctance to be physically close (though this can depend on a lot of things), being ambivalent about or not making plans, cadence of messaging decreasing as you are getting closer, or reluctance to incorporate a partner into their lives. Another clue that someone might have avoidant-attachment is if they go along with everything and "never fight." It might seem like they are just easygoing, but most people will have their own opinions and desires. If a partner never expresses an opinion in opposition to yours, it is likely because they don't want conflict. Avoidant partners will often keep dating/sleeping with someone even if they don't see a future because they don't know how to communicate that they would rather break up. Many examples of this are on *Love Is Blind*, if I may recommend a show! I discuss this more in depth in later chapters, but you get the gist. It is overall very difficult to have a close, intimate, vulnerable relationship with someone with avoidant attachment.

Anxious/preoccupied attachment:

The preoccupied/anxiously attached babies showed distress even before their caregivers were gone, were not easily comforted by the stranger (or comforted at all), and difficult or impossible to comfort even when the caregiver returned. The hypothesis behind this is that the baby cannot trust that the caregiver will return, and thus is not confident in their secure base. They cannot relax and explore because they are worried their caregiver won't return and they won't get their needs met.

In adulthood with romantic relationships, this can show up in key ways as well. Lots of calling, texting, reassurance seeking, etc. Getting very upset if someone doesn't respond right away. Obsessing over lots of details, wondering if they are indicators of withdrawing/someone not liking them. It is very hard for the anxious-attachment partner to leave things "unresolved." They often want to talk about everything, which is healthy in one sense, but if they are unable to let things sit for a bit, this is a sign of anxious attachment. If they are secure in the relationship, they are okay with someone taking a minute to process, and they don't take it as a signal that their partner might want out. That is the fear: that their partner will leave them, and they do everything they can to ensure that that is not the case. This can be a bit much when it comes to adult relationships. They have a hard time giving their partner space; for example, if they just want to decompress. They might also take sexual rejection very hard/personally, even though someone might just be tired. They see it as a rejection of them and get anxious about the state of the relationship. *Love is Blind* is also chock-full of anxiously attached people!

Disorganized attachment:

This style of attachment does not fall into any of the above categories and was characterized in the experiments by overt displays of fear, jerky movements, and disassociation. Many of the infants displayed both anxious and avoidant behaviors. The researchers learned that most of the caregivers of these infants had suffered trauma shortly after or during the birth of the babies.

In adulthood, this can also play out in disorganized ways, where sometimes a person will respond anxiously and sometimes avoidantly to a threat of abandonment. Part of them wants a close relationship, but they are afraid of intimacy. This style of attachment is often the result of trauma and massively un-met needs in childhood, or very inconsistent caregiving. This style is unpredictable and very difficult in adult relationships because it is marked by instability.

HOW DO DIFFERENT ATTACHMENT STYLES INTERACT?

In a securely attached partnership, both partners are confident in what they bring to the table and are comfortable verbalizing their needs, feeling vulnerable, being physically intimate, etc. I don't see much of this pairing in therapy because they are doing pretty well! When I do see a securely attached couple, they are usually coming in with a pretty specific issue, and they are in and out of therapy in a handful of sessions. They both are onboard with therapy, they take feedback and suggestions well, they introspect, and they try different things! I had one couple come to me asking for help navigating an upcoming transition to overseas due to a Foreign Service position (this is DC therapy, after all). They had two small children as well and wanted help anticipating what might come up with this big life change. They were both motivated and a joy to work with. They were open-minded, didn't get defensive, learned how to be more supportive of each other, and got more physically connected.

In an anxious-anxious relationship, there is a lot of.... Anxiety! Surprise. Both people are worried about losing the other person, and this manifests in overcommunication (yes, this is a thing. Not EVERY feeling needs to be discussed/addressed. Sometimes you have to deal with it internally) and potentially a lot of drama. This is the couple that might come to therapy while they are dating, basically at the drop of a hat.

In contrast, the avoidant-avoidant pairing doesn't talk about much. It might seem on the outside like it is a great relationship because there is little to no fighting, but in reality, problems are often swept under the rug. This is typically a pretty unhappy relationship because neither person is getting their needs met. I don't see many of this pairing either, because they are both so avoidant and don't want to come to therapy, unless things get dire. It is usually very hard to come back from years of avoidance, hurt, and pent-up resentment that is usually present in this dynamic.

Lastly, and the most common pairing I see in therapy, is the anxious-avoidant, or pursuer-distancer. The anxious partner is the one who reaches out for therapy, and is often the one that has "tried" in the past. However, the more the anxious person pursues, the more the avoidant withdraws, which sets the pursuer into panic that they will be abandoned. One paradigm of attachment research involved a mom engaging with her baby (laughing, smiling, cooing, etc.,), and then all of a sudden going completely expressionless. This sent the baby into complete panic mode, and she tried anything to get mom's attention. As soon as mom re-engaged, the baby calmed down. This is also a version of stonewalling (refer back to the four horsemen). This withdrawal is intolerable for the anxiously-attached person, while simultaneously the anxiety is intolerable for the withdrawer, who cannot handle the emotional intensity and the perceived pressure and withdraws more. Eventually, the pursuer gets "pursuer fatigue," which is a result of repeated rejection, and also withdraws. Then, the dynamic becomes more like the avoidant-avoidant.

CAN ATTACHMENT STYLES CHANGE?

Yes! People who have an insecure attachment style can change. I've definitely seen insecurely attached partners change to secure attachment with therapy. Also, changing the relationship status also can provide opportunities for a change in attachment style. Once people are out of a relationship that was insecure, there is a lot of room for this. Your attachment style might also be different in different relationships; you might be the pursuer (anxious-attachment) if you are with an avoidant partner, and vise-versa. For every withdrawer that can come forward more, there is a pursuer that needs to take a step back and learn to deal with their anxiety. This is how attachment styles change. With an understanding of your upbringing and your current attachment style, you can introspect and learn strategies to change your patterns. Consider if you have been avoidant. It will likely be anxiety-provoking to learn how to be vulnerable, confront issues, and ask for what you want. This is where therapy can help. If you are anxious, it will behoove you to learn how to sit with your anxiety and not seek reassurance constantly. Introspecting about your attachment style could bring up some traumatic things from your upbringing, which is why therapy could be useful! But yes, you can surely become a securely attached person and find other securely attached people! This goes for all relationships by the way, not just romantic relationships. Secure people attract secure people. Aim for this moving forward. In addition to therapy, taking time to focus on yourself and develop your sense-of-self (more on this in the next chapter) after your divorce can also change your attachment style to be more secure. If you are comfortable and confident in yourself, you will be more at peace with your own company, and not get into relationships driven by insecure attachment. Consider this analogy: You find yourself unemployed. If you have $1 in your bank account, you will be desperate to find a job because you are financially insecure and not in a position to be choosy. But if you have $30K in your checking and several hundred thousand as a cushion in savings, investments, etc., you are much freer to find a job that is the right fit, and you would be looking for a job based on that, not based on desperation to find anything that will pay you. Same thing with secure attachment: if you work on yourself first, you will enter into future relationships for the "right reasons."

IF YOU'VE EVER BEEN TOLD YOU NEED MORE EMPATHY...

You are not alone. I see lots of men in my practice whose partners complain they are not empathetic or not sensitive. This is where a lot of attachment injury comes from, when people feel they are not heard/understood, and this is very damaging. Empathy is definitely an inherent quality that can vary widely, but it can also be learned. Putting yourself in the mind of someone else is a skill that requires perspective taking and practice. Of course, you can work on this in therapy, but there are other ways to do that as well. Any opportunity you have to see the world through other people's eyes is an opportunity to build empathy. Even something like reading a novel or watching a show can expand your worldview and perspective. If a partner has ever suggested reading something she is reading or watching something she is watching, often this might be a reason behind that. She wants to share an emotional experience with you. Often, avoidantly-attached people will avoid this type of emotional content because of the emotions and vulnerability that may accompany it. This is also where the change is. You can learn to deepen your emotions and feel vulnerable and safe, which can ultimately lead to more intimacy and connection.

TL;DR:

- There are different attachment styles based on your upbringing and they matter.
- Attachment styles play out in adult relationships.
- People who are securely attached are confident, vulnerable, and communicate effectively.
- Avoidant-attachment individuals have great difficulty with vulnerability and intimacy.
- Anxious/preoccupied attached individuals have a deep fear of abandonment.
- Disorganized attached individuals often have a history of trauma and can be unpredictable.
- Different attachment styles interact differently.
- Attachment styles can change! You can become a securely attached person, depending on the relationship.
- Therapy can increase empathy, but so can things you can do on your own such as reading novels or watching shows.

HOMEWORK

☐ Introspect about your attachment style, your upbringing, and the dynamic in your marriage.

☐ Take an attachment quiz online! There are so many; just google and you will find one. Or, you might know it after reading this chapter; it actually is not rocket science.

☐ Time to get moving on that empathy! Pick a novel or a show and get into it!

CHAPTER 7

I WANT TO BE MY BEST SELF

What to Work On Before You Start Dating

"Honey, no offense, but your breath..."
—SAMANTHA TO BERNIE TURTLETAUB (A ROMANTIC PROSPECT)

"I know. It's these Chinese herbs I'm taking. You know, for longer life." —BERNIE TURTLETAUB

"Well, with breath like that, you're gonna live a very long life... alone." —SAMANTHA

Bad breath! Total non-starter. And bad hygiene in general. This particular situation in the show does not turn out well because, as it turns out, you really can't change someone. They have to want to change/improve on their own! It often takes someone's world being rocked to do that. So, here we are. This chapter will guide you through some specific areas for self-improvement that will likely help you on the dating market, but truly are ultimately for YOU and building your confidence, esteem, and sense of self post-divorce. It is likely that some of your sense of self has been lost (or maybe if you really introspect, you aren't sure if you ever actually had a strong one) and having a strong sense of self leads to confidence and self-love. Of course, therapy can help with deep insecurities but so can these very practical tips!

I'm sure you are already swiping and have likely gone on dates and maybe have had other situationships/relationships. That's fine; just know you are probably not in a position to jump into anything serious if you are actually still in the divorce process. In fact, it is completely normal to need 1-2 years after your divorce is final to be in a position to seriously date. Be honest with yourself first and foremost (and other people of course) about that (more on this in the next chapter). For now, at least try to focus on some of the following things before you jump online and get sucked up in the sea of dopamine. I obviously had two chapters dedicated to therapy, so this one focuses on other stuff. Bear with me if this comes off as "mean mommy." These things are important, and I'll put her away after this chapter.

PHYSICAL HEALTH: If you haven't been on top of doctors' visits, there is no time like the present! Schedule a physical and go to the dentist. Get all your bloodwork done. If anything is not optimal, address it. Take vitamins, testosterone (if low), etc. You might be surprised by how many mood issues can be addressed by getting bloodwork done and addressing the issue (energy, sex drive, etc.). Guys, look, I know this seems basic. But I have heard so many women complain about these things. The bottom line is—taking care of yourself is attractive and sexy and sends a signal that you are ready to take care of someone else! If there are kids in the picture, this is obviously a good motivator to be on top of your physical health. Think back on your marriage—did your wife complain about you not taking care of yourself? If so, really think about this. Don't write her off as overbearing and "momming" you. Where there is smoke, my friend. She might have been "momming" you, but it doesn't mean there wasn't some truth to it, and don't get in your own way of getting healthy. It is possible this was a pattern early in your relationship; she might have even scheduled appointments for you. This is co-dependence and not a good move for either party, but in the beginning there was probably a draw for this. Over time, this dynamic becomes much less appealing as life becomes harder and both people need to be taken care of in different ways. Anyway, this is a great time for a regular exercise routine (classes, walks, hiking, yoga, etc.). Start really small if this is overwhelming (10 pushups/day, taking the stairs, short walks, looking into fitness classes/gyms nearby or even just fitness apps).

Another important category under physical health is reproductive health. If you do not want kids or more kids and are sure of this, strongly consider getting a vasectomy if you don't already have one. This is a simple way to make things much easier going forward into the dating world. It is an easy way to a.) put all your cards on the table by making it pretty clear where you stand on that, and b.) and make sure there is no accidental pregnancy. Condoms are still super important (I talk about this later), but this at least removes one important risk.

CLOTHES/GROOMING: Okay, guys, throw away the boxers. Please. With love, you are not a teenager. While you are at it, please throw away any clothes with holes and/or stains, and ones that don't fit you well (like hanging off). You don't have to get a totally new wardrobe, but truly consider investing in at least some new items! If you need help, there are professionals. You can go with a styling service like Stitch Fix or Trunk Club, or you can hire a personal stylist, just to get a head start. You can also go to thrift stores and get really nice things on the cheap. Remember, this is the beginning of your new life, and your style should reflect that! Also, get a haircut and whatever other grooming might be necessary (trimming ear hair, nose hair, etc.).

A WORD ON HYGIENE: Oh, how important (as Samantha pointed out). A lot of women are Highly Sensitive People (HSPs). HSPs are more sensitive to external stimuli (light, sound, smell) as well as internal stimuli (pain, hunger). They often have higher anxiety and are more disturbed by the environment. You can read more about this in Elaine Aron's book *The Highly Sensitive Person: How to Thrive When the World Overwhelms You*. Think back for a moment: if your wife complained about a lot of noise, or being cold a lot, or was overwhelmed by playdates, loud music, etc., she might be an HSP. Learning more about this will help you understand where she was coming from with these complaints, as well as help you to understand future potential partners. This relates to hygiene BECAUSE a lot of women are very sensitive to smells and turned off by odors (and conversely, turned ON by nice smells). This is a common reason why women don't want to have sex (much more to come on this topic), so please make sure you are smelling wonderful everywhere (this includes brushing your teeth). A woman doesn't have to be an HSP to be bothered by poor hygiene, by the way. Most women are, just less so than HSPs.

BOOZE (and other substances/addictive behaviors): Big topic. Dating apps these days often have people categorizing the frequency of their drinking ("often," "socially on weekends," "never," etc.). Obviously, since people tend to want to paint themselves in the best light, the answer to this question might not reflect the actual truth. This is a real opportunity to think deeply about your drinking/substance use habits. Some questions to consider: Are you drinking several times a week? Do you look forward to a drink after your kids go to bed? Did your wife complain about it? Did you fight about it? In general, women do not like it when their male partners drink. Let me explain why! It is NOT because she doesn't want you to have a good time, or she wants to control you, as you might think. You might also not be bothered by her drinking, so you might deem her protests invalid. But here's the thing (and there are exceptions of course, like if your wife herself had a heavy drinking problem): when she gets tipsy or even drunk, this is likely not a safety concern for you in the same way it is for her. She relies on you to be able to take care of her and the kids (if applicable) from a safety perspective, and if you are in an altered state of mind, she cannot rely on you in the same way and this makes her anxious (or it exacerbates pre-existing levels of anxiety). If something happened and you needed to spring to action, you wouldn't be able to. So, she did not feel relaxed and comfortable with you. She is also not turned on by you being drunk, as you are probably less in control. Maybe you are louder/more aggressive, more sexual, funnier (though not to her), etc. Also, smelling like booze is a turn-off. You might not have the same issues with your wife when she drinks, so it might be hard for you to understand her beef. This is all to say, don't brush off your ex-wife's issues with your drinking. So, in your journey to be your best self, think about your alcohol use. A (small) handful of drinks in one week is probably a good goal. If this seems impossible, you know what I am going to say by now... find a good therapist to help or visit your local (or Zoom local) AA meeting. Many people have also had success with SMART Recovery (a CBT approach to substance use treatment). As you are re-entering (or entering) the dating market, you will find that women who are also divorced or who are otherwise experienced in relationships/life in general, will have an eye on this.

There are other areas of addictive behaviors to consider. Gambling, sex, and pornography are all issues that I see a lot of men struggle with. I have a whole chapter on porn later in the book, and several chapters about sex (complicated!), but if you think you have an issue with either one of these- you are not alone. Sports gambling is also very common these days (gambling was added to the DSM-5 as an addictive behavior). Introspect about your relationship with these behaviors, and consider help if you have struggled. If your wife- or anyone else- has mentioned these, again- it is something to consider.

YOUR HOME: Okay. Huge. Mazel tov, you are now the agent of your living space. Your home should be a place where you feel relaxed and comfortable, and somewhere that is reflective of your personal style. My mom always says, "Rome wasn't built in a day," and she is right! It takes time to build it, but start taking small steps. Focus on one room or project at a time. For instance, get new bedding and towels. When Miranda (SATC, of course, still not sorry) gets new sheets, she says, "if you build it, he will come," and then wonders if "everything [she] brings into this bedroom has to have a flaw" when there is a snag on her new "Peach Florentine" sheets. I have heard many stories from clients and friends about newly separated or divorced men's homes, and they are either very turned off, or very turned ON by the state of them.

If you have kids, and depending on their ages, let them pick out stuff for their room(s) and other parts of the house. You definitely want them to feel at home in your home, whether it is a completely new space or you stayed in the home. If the latter, it is almost more important for it to feel like it is a reflection of you, and not just the leftovers from your married life. In her book, *This American Ex-Wife*, Lyz Lenz discussed how she bought a house and let her kids paint the walls in the basement so that they knew it was their home too. I love that. If there is a way to create that autonomy and magic for them, definitely do so! I will discuss more about kids in a later chapter.

FINANCES: Separating your finances (which I know can take some time and be complicated) is a pretty important step toward feeling independent. This might be the first time ever you don't have to think about the impact of your spending on someone else (besides kids, obviously)! Finances might have been a point of contention in your marriage, and if so, introspect on this. It can be very liberating to be the agent of your own finances, but if this was a source of conflict, as I always advise, consider the source. Did you have very divergent attitudes about spending and saving? Did one of you prefer to stay in 5-star hotels while the other preferred to save that money and stay in a 3-star? Like most things, our attitudes about these things are shaped by our upbringings. So, what did you learn about finances growing up? You might have also managed the finances; in which case you are probably used to it. If not, you can (and should) learn! Consult financial experts if you need some guidance. Consulting experts is a big theme of mine, as you will see. Big fan of the outsource.

CUSTODY SCHEDULE: Obviously, if you don't have kids, you have my blessing to skip this section. If you have kids, make sure you have your custody situation mostly figured out or very close to it. Of course things come up that will require change/flexibility, but this is a signal that things are predictable and reliable, and you can actually plan things with a new partner (women like planning! And follow-through). I often hear men complain about women who like planning as being uptight. No. If you want to date someone who has their shit together, this woman is going to plan. This does not mean she cannot be flexible. But regarding custody, it's nice to know that things are relatively set. Now, of course things will come up and flexibility, especially with kids, is definitely a green flag. An example of flexibility: *"Hey, I know we talked about brunch with friends on Sunday, but my daughter really wants to go to this birthday party and her mom can't take* *her. Do you mind if we raincheck or pick another activity? I was really looking forward to it."* This is a signal that it is important to you to take your kid to a birthday party, and you are okay switching things up. Flexibility is NOT: *"I can't make plans because I have no idea what my schedule will be and can't you just go with the flow??"* If this is your life, perhaps the serious dating can wait a bit.

FRIENDS: I know it is not easy to make friends as an adult male. You may have lost some friends in the divorce if your wife was mostly the social event planner. But this is a time where it is really important to expand your social circle. Attend meet-ups. Go out in the world. Try to plan social events with colleagues. Ask other dads to do things with the kids when you have them. Take walks, ride your bike, sit at a bar, etc. If you have a niche hobby, go to Reddit to see if there are people in your area to do it with. I've had clients who have made friends that way. One client found a friend to help do contract work on his house, and another found a connection to help work on his car. There are support groups for divorced men as well! Look into those in your city. There are ways to connect with new people, and even though it might be a muscle you haven't exercised in a while, now is the time.

RELIGION/SPIRITUALITY: This can also be a time to connect/reconnect to religious/spiritual roots. A lot of people find comfort in a religious or spiritual practice. This could mean anything from solo meditation to joining or re-joining a faith-based community. Of course this also could be a great way to meet people, but that could just be an added bonus.

TO SUM UP

Honestly, everything that I mentioned above is ultimately for YOU. Figuring out who you are and what you want outside of your ex-wife will make you feel confident and secure, and be a good example for your kids (if applicable). It will make you feel like you truly have your shit together, and that you can actually offer something to a partner. You will feel empowered to make decisions on your own and feel confident in doing so. It will build your sense of self. This will feel especially good if you feel like you didn't have agency in your marriage. You might have been drawn to this for specific reasons (of course, often based in family of origin). Introspect about why you might have been drawn to a situation where you were not comfortable asserting yourself. You may have learned that one parent (not necessarily the woman) had a "my way or the highway" approach, and you learned that this is how marriage is. The more you set yourself up for confidence and independence, the more you are setting the stage for a truly equal partnership. You might think that women want to get their way all the time, but this is not true. Women are attracted to confident men who are NICE, and also respect their intelligence and decision-making. This is all to say, you have choices and agency to decide how to set up your new life, and it is exciting! Let your home, your hobbies, your wardrobe, etc., reflect that. Attracting a compatible partner is icing on the cake of you feeling good and confident in yourself.

TL;DR

- In a very kind and loving way, get your shit together. This will attract the type of woman that you want to date, but more importantly, it will increase your confidence!
- You have agency over so much of your life now, use it.
- Be healthy, smell nice.

- Set up a warm home that reflects you and your taste. Involve your kids (if applicable).

HOMEWORK

☐ Pick ONE of these areas and get started on it! Remember, small steps.

☐ If the drinking/substance use section resonated with you, introspect about it and consider taking some steps to address it.

CHAPTER 8

SWIPE RIGHT, SWIPE LEFT
Navigating Online Dating and Meeting New People

"Dear single..."
—CARRIE, READING A NEWSPAPER AD ALOUD TO THE GIRLS

"Single? You don't even have a name?" —MIRANDA

"Well, I'm single I don't deserve one." —CARRIE

"That's the postal equivalent of a drive-by shooting." —SAMANTHA

"Yeah and I thought those fifty-seven menus I get every day from Hunan Munan were annoying." —CARRIE

"Look at this! 'Don't let your soul mate slip away.'" —MIRANDA

"Oh, I know it's almost a threat like 'we have 'em he's just waiting for you but hurry 'cause he's slipping, slipping away, Oops there he goes.' Soulmates only exist in the Hallmark aisle." —CARRIE

"I disagree, I believe that there's that one perfect person out there to complete you." —CHARLOTTE

"And if you don't find him, what? You're incomplete?, it's so dangerous!" —MIRANDA

"Alright, first of all, the idea that there's only one out there, I mean, why don't I just shoot myself right now? I'd like to think that people have more than one soulmate." —CARRIE

"I agree, I've had hundreds." —SAMANTHA

"Yeah, and you know what, if you miss one along comes another, like cabs." —CARRIE

"No, that is not how it works." —CHARLOTTE

"Oh, okay." —CARRIE

I n this scene, the girls are discussing Carrie's dating service application that she received via snail mail (can you imagine??). They discuss Carrie's identity being reduced to "single" (a major topic of discussion throughout the series for all of them) and the topic of soulmates. I often think about what the series would have been like if there were dating apps. But for our purposes, we will discuss dating in 2024!

Okay, so you're contemplating Tinder. This CAN be seen as a positive sign, one that means you can envision the possibility of being with someone who is not your ex. Or, it could mean that you are—understandably—probably a bit lonely and horny and you think you can find solace in swiping. Here's the thing— really introspect about where you are at in terms of what you are looking for. If you are still separated or very recently divorced, you are likely not in a place for something serious, and you probably won't be for a while. If you are dating, a good barometer for readiness for something more serious is how you handle rejection. Not matching, someone not responding, rejection after a date or several dates...this will all happen. If you have low confidence/esteem, you will take this very hard. If you have worked on yourself and have become more confident/secure, you know it is not a big deal if someone rejects you, and it's just not a fit! You won't take it personally or spiral. This takes time and practice. Like I said in the last chapter, it takes probably 1-2 years after your divorce is final to settle into a new life and truly be in a place to contemplate a serious relationship. Until then, casual is the way to go. Which, by the way, is totally fine! Just be up-front about it. Honesty and directness are a turn-on, and you will actually probably attract more people if you tell them exactly what you are and are not looking for. Of course, this requires self-awareness on your part (refer back to why a therapist would be helpful right now!). I actually encourage transparent casual dating in order for you to get to know yourself and what you are looking for. However—major caveat—if you have kids, do not have a revolving door of dates that your kids meet. Date in your kid-free time. More on when to introduce kids in a later chapter, but for now, at this point in your post-married life, limit your dating to your kid-free time.

In this chapter, I will discuss dating apps, including how to set up your profile, tips for chatting, things to look for, and other ways to meet people. If you already are on the apps, cool. Hopefully, you'll still find some helpful tips here.

WHAT APP TO CHOOSE

When you are ready to swipe, which app should you pick? There are so many dating apps to choose from! Truthfully, it doesn't really matter which one(s) you land on. Unless you have a real niche (Jswipe, Christian Mingle, Stir, Feeld, Grindr (if you reallyyy want to start exploring) etc.), they are generally the same, and the content on your profile is the important part. Generally, Hinge, Bumble, and Tinder are the big ones. Hinge and Bumble are more geared toward relationships (but still have the option for "casual"), whereas Tinder is more for hook-ups. OK Cupid is another one. It matches you based on a compatibility rating, which is a cool feature. There really are so many, but I wouldn't advise having more than 2-3 at a time.

SETTING UP YOUR PROFILE

So, how do you set up your profile? This might be intimidating, but no worries, you got this. A few things to keep in mind. Be your full authentic self. That is the most important! You want to find a good FIT, even if you aren't looking for anything serious. Trust me, aside from not hurting people (that minor detail, right?), the more up-front you are, the more time and stress you will save yourself down the line, and the more genuine and authentic you are, the more you will attract the best people for you. If you are "figuring out your dating goals" (an option on Hinge), say that!! No shame. You can be 45 years old and still figuring it out (as many people are post-divorce), again, as long as you are upfront about it. Women actually do pay attention to what you put in the "looking for" category on these apps (several clients have told me I've been right after they discovered this on their own). Most apps will have you pick what you are looking for, so please do introspect and be honest about it. Do this, and you will attract someone who either also wants the same thing or is okay with what you are looking for. I have a whole section later on "DTR" (defining the relationship), but for now, just choose what feels the most closely aligned with your dating goals at the moment. You can always change it. Of course, if you don't know what to put, a good therapist can help you consider what you are looking for!

Okay, profiles. Make sure you fill out all of the fields they ask because most of them include pretty important dealbreakers (such as wanting kids, politics, religion, etc.). Be upfront and let people decide for themselves what they are looking for. Next, photos. Don't be the guy with the cliché photos on the apps! No holding fish (unless this is really an active hobby of yours, but even that it is pretty cliché tbh!), NO gym selfies (even if this is an active hobby of yours). No car selfies!! Put photos of yourself wearing normal clothes (i.e. something you would wear on a date, like a sweater or a T-shirt and jeans). If you don't have any, ask your friends to take some when you are out. Put photos of JUST you. It is assumed that you have friends—don't open yourself up for comparisons. Your first photo should be a clear picture of your face; no sunglasses or other obstructions. Smile in your photos! Try to look kind and approachable. I can't believe I have to say this, but I do: Do NOT have photos of you flicking off the camera. It is truly bananas that this is a thing. Also, no costumes. They aren't sexy. You should have several full body shots (where it is VERY clear what your body looks like), and try to have a few of you doing something you are actually into. For example, if you actively play music, have a photo or two of you doing that. The exception to this is gym photos: you might be an active gym-goer, but these are sleazy for dating apps. If you work out, she will learn that soon. Also, don't have photos of you hiking if you hiked one time 10 years ago. Try to have recent photos, but at the very least make sure they look like you! Ask a friend or family member (or therapist! I have helped many clients choose their dating profile pictures) to look at your photos if you aren't sure they look like you. You do not want your date to be surprised when you meet (as you wouldn't want to be). If you don't have good recent photos, consider outsourcing this as well. I had a client who hired a task rabbit for $60 to take photos of him specifically for dating apps. So smart! This shows you are taking it seriously and making an effort.

Accurately represent every aspect of yourself (height, age, etc.). Put your accurate marital status (divorced, separated). Integrity is sexy! Don't put a different age to sneak through filters and then claim "the app won't let me change it." Let people screen out if they want to; it's their prerogative. If people have age cutoffs, height cutoffs, religious requirements, whatever else... who cares. If you are bald, do not have hats in every photo. Have enough confidence to know that they are missing out on you, and focus on the ones who want you just as you are. Obviously, people will find out about your height and hair status when you meet, so just be upfront! I have clients who have been told at the end of dates that their date is eight years older than they said, or shown up to meet someone who is four inches shorter, or thirty pounds heavier. Misleading someone is a waste of everyone's time and takes away agency for people to choose for themselves because it is withholding information. You might not think something is important (i.e. age or height), but a prospective partner might, so let them decide by providing all the information. Remember, there is a lid for every pot, so just be you!

This leads me to my next point: just in general, do not try to make yourself more interesting for the sake of the apps. Choose a few key things about you and highlight those things, but don't make things up, and don't exaggerate your interests in them just because you think you need to be more exciting. You are enough! If you genuinely want to get more involved in activities/hobbies for YOU (of course this is a good idea; refer to previous chapter), but don't do it for the profile.

So, what should you highlight? What are the things that make you uniquely you? Think of a handful of keywords that, taken together, really embody yourself and no one else. For example, if I picked five things to highlight about myself, I would pick: yoga, musicals, reality TV, psychologist, mom. I would not pick: NYT crosswords, rock-climbing, global politics. Why? Because even though they might sound "more interesting" than reality TV (though of course they aren't); they aren't me! I would want someone who appreciates the same things, and digs the person I am because I am into what I'm into. If someone doesn't think your five "things" are interesting to them or a good fit, then they aren't for you! You don't have to necessarily be into all the same things, but there should be SOME overlap. More on compatibility later. A quick word on all this in the context of a divorce. This might be another area where your esteem is affected, and you don't feel like you have much to bring to the table. This is a great opportunity to find the things that you are into and showcase them, AND it is also a great opportunity to learn that you are enough just the way you are. I promise people will find you interesting. Money back guarantee. Not really. But you know.

Different apps have different formats, so, there are many ways to let your personality shine! Some apps require baseline info, but add more on top of it. Don't do the bare minimum. Dating coach Erika (@alittlenudge) always says "Lazy bio= lazy dater," and I agree. Also, be positive in your bio. Talk about what you bring to the table and the type of person you want to attract. Here are a few examples of pretty good bios:

"Guitar player, yogi, and small business owner in Baltimore. I love to cook. I love to hike. I love to learn. I have one kid and I value friendship, family, and adventures."

"Movies, live music, dive bars, noodles, and arts with some pre-fix menus, dancing, and travel mixed in."

If you are on an app that has prompts, like Hinge or Tinder, choose a mix of funny and serious ones. I'm sure you are hilarious, but most women appreciate a serious side as well. Some apps (like Hinge) even have the option for voice memos—use this! My personal favorite method of communication, and it's a great way to get to know someone. You can really show your personality/humor that way.

You want to avoid statements about what you are not looking for and just general negativity. Here are some examples of what NOT to put:

"Trump supporters swipe left"

"Is anyone on here real??"

"Well, I'm on tinder, so things aren't going great"

"Don't be [a single mom, religious, high maintenance], etc."

"If you can't bother with anything more than 'hi,' keep swiping"

While the above might be true to what you are looking for, they scream negativity and/or challenging off the bat. Speak positively about what you ARE looking for, not about what you are not looking for. Everything will reveal itself in time (and that time could be as early as an initial message), meaning that you will get to see what is compatible and what is not with more experience.

SWIPING AND CHATTING

Now you're all ready to swipe and message, mazel tov.

A word of warning for fake profiles: They exist and you'll probably learn pretty quickly who is real and who isn't. If they look like a 19-year-old model with a ton of filters and no information in their bio, it's a good bet they are fake. I'm sure you are sexy, but be realistic about your prospects. Here are several other tells:

- If they want to move the conversation off the app immediately (i.e. to WhatsApp, Telegram, kik, Signal. Telegram and kik are especially red flags because they do not require a phone number, just a username).

- If they ask for more pictures without offering any of their own.

- If they offer more pictures (including nudes) very quickly.

- If they try to draw very personal information from you that you don't feel comfortable sharing very quickly (i.e. work or family related. This is a "trust your gut" type thing).

- Refusing or delaying using the video feature on the app (if it has it. More on video chats in a bit).

- If they unmatch after you decline a suggestion for chatting off the app, they likely were not real.

- If they have photos that look like screenshots (either from other apps or social media).

- If they have only their social media information on their profile.

- If they make any reference to Only Fans (google this if you aren't familiar), Cashapp, Venmo, or any website or service basically.

- Lastly, if they drop any very heavy handed hints about wanting to be spoiled, wanting a generous man, generous older man, love language is gifts, or anything else along those lines.

Here's the bottom line on fake profiles: Keep the above examples in mind but also trust your gut.

Regarding real people, err on the side of casting a wide net when you swipe and then you can be more discerning when you chat. All the major dealbreakers will come out when you chat/get to know someone, so you can bow out at any time. The easiest things to weed out are the most obvious ones. For example, if someone wants kids and you don't want kids. Beyond major dealbreakers (also more to come on this), I encourage an open mind! You never know who you might click with. If you are curious about someone at all, see if you match! Swipe right on people you find interesting and attractive, and who seem similar to you.

The more I learn from professional and personal experience, compatibility is so important. I keep coming back to this theme. You can discern compatibility on an app from fairly early on. There are even fields for personality types! You obviously won't be exactly the same (and don't need to be), but the more similar you are on many dimensions (extraversion/introversion, religious affiliation or lack thereof, political views, love languages, hobbies, music, preferred cuisine, etc.), the EASIER things will be and the more you can understand and empathize with each other. So, look to see if the person you are swiping on is similar to you! Are their photos of activities you would enjoy? Do you laugh at their prompts (yes, actually read them!)? Are you attracted to them (so important, more on this later)? Do they talk about partying and you go to bed early, or vise-versa? Is their "typical Sunday" something you would hate? Does she talk about reality TV, and you wouldn't be caught dead watching it? These are all important questions! Some apps (OK Cupid) even have compatibility ratings, where you answer a bunch of questions and it gives ratings of compatibility (don't match with someone who is rated 60% compatible). In my experience, it is not true that "opposites attract." Think back on your marriage. What areas were you compatible and incompatible? I have a friend who is an avid runner. He is married and met his wife in college, and she is not a runner. They have a strong and loving marriage, but he has talked about the fact that if he were dating now, he would probably only date runners. It just makes it easier. People who are super into food and love all types of cuisine probably should not date vegans, or people who are not foodies. And so on. These are things you can tell from the apps pretty early. Since compatibility is a recurring theme in the book, I won't take more time in this section, but you get the idea. Swipe on people who seem to be similar to you.

It's a match! Now what?? Here are some do's and don'ts of on-line messaging:

DO :

- Send a first message; this signals interest and intent.

- Say something friendly and positive!

- Comment on a photo or a prompt, and ask a question or say something about it. For example, if it is a scenic photo, ask about where it was taken or comment that you have been or that it is on your list.

- You CAN give a compliment that is not too heavy-handed (and not about her body. For example, "you have great eyes," or "I love your smile!"). Caveat to this: This has to be done very carefully. Women deal with unwanted comments on their physical appearance all the time, so it is often not welcome on dating apps, even if they are lighter compliments. On the other hand, if it feels genuine to you, you should do it. She can decide if it is welcome or not.

- Say something that reflects the fact that you actually read her profile.

- Attempt to connect via video, phone, or IRL sooner rather than later (as schedules allow). Do this after a few messages are exchanged. Women hate a "pen pal" situation, and most appreciate a first move.

- Stay on the app until you have met in person. Plan a date on the app and give your phone number the day before once it is already set as a contingency. Coach Erika says that dates are much more likely to happen this way, and I tend to agree. You can weed out people who might text endlessly back and forth. Exceptions to this are video chats (if it can't be done through the app).

DON'T:

- Just "like" a photo or prompt; say something to start the conversation.

- Comment on her body.

- Ask for more photos. You have to be willing to take some risks with online dating; she may not look exactly like her pictures (though I always encourage everyone to post clear full-body shots).

- Ask any variation of: "why are you still single", "what's a girl like you doing on Tinder", etc. In fact, don't ever ask a woman why she is still single. The answer is likely because she is waiting for the right fit and might be insulted by that question. It is also getting very personal very quickly, and there is time for that.

- Along those lines, don't ask very personal questions too soon (for example, "why did your relationship end?").

- Turn the conversation sexual.

If you want to meet, don't chat for too long. All will be revealed as you get to know each other in person, so please pay special attention to the penultimate bullet point above. Revealing too much via text sets expectations high for in-person connections and can give a false sense of intimacy. Once you have had a few back-and-forths, make an effort to connect quickly either in person, or via phone or facetime. Present the option for a low-key date (coffee, a walk, or a drink), and offer to continue chatting for a bit or connecting via phone first. This shows that you are mindful that someone's preferences might be to chat a bit longer before meeting. I often recommend a video-chat before meeting in person. Though it is not ideal and can be awkward, the benefits of this are twofold: One, you can save a lot of time, energy, and money if you don't click with the person and don't want to meet IRL, and two, if you do click, you might be even more excited to meet. If a woman suggests it, always do it. There are certain challenges in online dating that are unique for women, and it is helpful to understand those.

A WORD ABOUT ONLINE DATING IN GENERAL

I will pause here to highlight some differences in online dating for men and women for the purposes of having more empathy and understanding for the women you are trying to date. For one, the risk of physical violence and sexual assault is higher for women. One 2022 study conducted by Julie Valentine and colleagues found that dating app facilitated sexual assault made up 8.02% of all sexual assault cases reviewed using forensic data. Men also tend to make the conversation sexual more quickly than women (don't do this), which makes women feel uncomfortable at best and violated and objectified at worst. Men send unsolicited pictures (consensual is fine, just please communicate about it!) at higher rates than women. Women and men can both get catfished, but when that happens, the risk of physical danger is higher for women. Of course, there is the risk of people lying about their age, marital status, religion, height, etc. One 2007 study found that 81% of participants lied about at least one characteristic on their online dating profiles, with women lying more about weight and men lying more about height. Not surprising of course. Anyway, I'm sharing this information because as men looking to date women online, it is important to be aware of and sensitive to the different challenges that women face.

In fact, the risk of online dating for women is high enough that there is now a social media group warning women against specific men. This "secret" (whoops) group is a platform where women, who are theoretically vetted to make sure they are in fact women (and not men posing as women to gain access to the group), can post men they are dating and ask tens of thousands (literally. The first group was over 80,000 members before it got shut down, and now it is about 60,000) of women if there is any "tea or red flags" on the guy. Then, women comment on what they know about this naïve man whose Hinge profile is posted for all women of that city to chime in on (there are several groups all around the country). Women can also post specific warnings about men they have dated, chatted with, married, etc. The group has been written up in the *Washington Post* and other media outlets and is fairly controversial. On the one hand, there was a literal murderer posted (pretty nice to know these minor red flags of homicide before swiping right), there have been posts about cheating married men, men who have lied about any number of characteristics, and general creeps. On the other hand, do men need to be publicly shamed for a pattern of unmatching? My personal opinion on this is mixed, but I think its existence is important enough to share in this book.

The bottom line is, there are definitely pros and cons to online dating in general. It is a tool that when used effectively, can be great. But you have to know what to look for and have a critical eye. Some pros include: Meeting people you never would otherwise meet, exercising the muscles of talking to people, asking someone out, flirting, and putting yourself out there. You get comfortable describing yourself and asking other people questions. You can be specific about what you are looking for. You learn how to tolerate rejection (this is so important for dating in general!). You can make new friends and different kinds of connections as well—you never know! You might "swipe right" on someone you never would be drawn to IRL and have a great connection.

On the other hand, dating apps can be quite time consuming. You will likely spend time meeting people you never would have been drawn to if you met IRL. There are lots of fake profiles, flakey people, and people who aren't serious. One might assume that just because someone is on an app means they are "ready to date"; this is a dangerous assumption. More cons: In-person chemistry is unpredictable, it can take a toll on your self-confidence, and can lead to dating burnout and cynicism if it is too time-consuming. You might not know how to represent yourself, you might be an awkward conversationalist, etc. So, while I do think it is an important tool to use if you want to meet people these days, there are other ways as well!

OTHER WAYS OF MEETING PEOPLE

Meeting IRL

Okay, that's cool too. I definitely encourage trying to meet IRL, as well as the apps. Being active in the world will be helpful during this time no matter what. Do things that you enjoy doing; that you would be doing anyway! You will be your best self when you are doing things that you enjoy. If you are forcing yourself to go to things just to meet people, it is not authentic and it puts too much pressure on the activity. Just get into the world for its own sake. While you are out, it doesn't hurt to make eye contact and smile and maybe start a conversation if you see someone you find attractive. Just don't be creepy (leering, continuing to talk after clear signals that someone isn't interested). Chat a bit about something benign (the weather- seriously), and see if there is a vibe. Women are socialized to be nice (ugh), so many women might talk and be nice and actually have no interest in you, and that's fine too. Rejection is part of the process (if the thought of rejection is so scary for you that it stops you from engaging...here's that therapy thing again). It's harder to meet people in the wild these days because a lot of people are on their phones, but just put down the phone and look around. If you sense interest/flirtation (I have more info on how to flirt in the next chapter), it's okay to take a risk and ask for their number, or their social media if that comes up (it IS 2024!). A lot of women appreciate a confident move, though like I mentioned, read the room. If you follow up and text and don't get anything back, or if she seems reticent to give it to you in the first place, that's, of course, a sign. Please pay attention to that. You could even write your number down on a piece of paper and give it to her, and leave the ball in her court. That is a great way to take the pressure off her responding in the moment. A major advantage of meeting IRL is assessing chemistry right away. It also forces you to think more about the importance of the qualities you think you might be looking for. For example, if you meet someone IRL and you are very drawn to them, it might not matter if she does or does not check certain boxes.

Matchmaking

Another way to meet people is by matchmaking. This is definitely a good way to have someone else do the legwork for you to find potential matches; however, there is no guarantee of chemistry as is the case with apps. However, if you are very serious about meeting someone (and I definitely encourage waiting on this option until you are), this could be a good way to go! This is definitely a good filter for people who are serious, as most people will not pay for pricey matchmaking services if they are not looking for a serious relationship. Many matchmakers also offer coaching along the way, which can of course be helpful! If this is appealing to you, investigate matchmakers in your area. There are online ones as well.

Set-ups

Ask to be set up. You can ask your friends, colleagues, friends of friends, etc. Basically put the word out that you are looking! Try not to be concerned that this is a "desperate" move, because it isn't! This is only "desperate" if you have super anxious-attachment and you fear being alone. When you are coming from a confident and secure place, this is totally legit! You can be nervous about being vulnerable, but it is important to do it anyway if you really want to meet people.

TL;DR

- Be self-aware of where you are in the dating process and what you are looking for (therapy can help with this, but this is a start!).
- Be your authentic self on the apps (this includes all demographic variables)! Do not misrepresent yourself. And don't use ChatGPT or AI for your profiles. Just be you!
- Look for compatibility. Do you connect with this person's vibe?
- There are many "do's and don'ts" of chatting on the apps.
- Meet quickly if you connect on the apps.
- Meeting IRL is possible too. Matchmaking and setups are also possibilities.

HOMEWORK

☐ Choose some photos and maybe set up a profile! If you already have one, consider if it needs tweaking after reading my sage advice. Ask for help if this is challenging.

SO, YOUR WIFE LEFT YOU... NOW WHAT?

CHAPTER 9

THE FIRST DATE PLAYBOOK

How to Make a Great Impression

"Well, you gotta take risks, so you don't wind up an old maid!!" —CHARLOTTE

"Must not wind up old maid, must not wind up old maid... how am I gonna remember that?? Anyone have a pen??" —CARRIE

This was a conversation after Carrie got stood up for a blind date and was complaining to the girls that she was done with dating. She talks about how she would much rather spend time with her friends than risk a bad time on a date. Samantha replies, "That's sweet, honey, but we're never gonna fuck you." This is just another example to highlight what dating can be like for BOTH men and women, in that it is always a risk of a bad evening. Time spent with someone that isn't a fit is certainly an inevitability of dating, so do your best to make it worth both of your time, but also if you learn from each experience, it's never a waste of time.

PLANNING A DATE

What should a first date be? Don't suggest involved, lengthy activities. You might have something fun and unique in mind like bowling or stand-up paddleboarding, but you don't want to get stuck in a situation where neither of you can extricate yourselves if you aren't feeling it. Save the more involved (and pricier activities) for second and third dates. The goal of a first date is to see if you enjoy each other's company and are attracted to each other (and want a second date). It should be short and—hopefully—sweet!

Here are some suggestions for short activities where you can actually get to know each other a bit:

- A drink (can also be mocktails if one or both of you doesn't drink alcohol).

- Meeting for coffee.

- A walk.

- A quick or light lunch (use work as an excuse to keep it short).

- You could suggest dinner, but sometimes women don't want to commit to a dinner before they know they like you.

So, suggest something easy and laid back, where you can talk. You could pose all of these as suggestions and see what she picks. Most women want someone who takes initiative/control but is also flexible. Lastly, offer to go somewhere close to where she lives (but not like, "can we go somewhere close to you so we can go back and fuck after"). An exception to the drink, coffee, or walk first date is if she asks you to do something specific (like an art show). If this is an activity you would like to do anyway, then definitely go. This shows you are open-minded and you would be interested in what she is interested in. But, if you would never do the activity she suggested, this might not be a fit, and perhaps suggest something else for a first date so you can see if you vibe.

Here is some wording you can use for suggesting a date (after you have picked a day): "How about [this place] at 7:30pm? I'm open to suggestions if you have somewhere else in mind or if a different time works!" This shows that you can take initiative and plan, but you are open to flexibility. When the arrangements are set, say, "Great! It's a date!" (also a suggestion by @alittlenudge). This way, there is no ambiguity regarding what it is. There is nothing more annoying than tentative plans ("Tuesday might work", etc.). Secure women on the receiving end of this will make plans on Tuesday and will not wait.

Then, unless you have been talking consistently and have already confirmed, make sure you confirm the day before or the MORNING of at the very latest, but day before is ideal ("Hey! Looking forward to seeing you tomorrow/later tonight at X time and Y place!").

FIRST DATE CONVOS AND FLIRTING

Okay, here you are! If you've taken my sage advice so far, you have a date and a place that has a good vibe where you can talk. You are wearing a clean shirt and your teeth are brushed! Yay! A note on attire: be comfortable. Your outfit should reflect who you are, but please do refer to my section on grooming/wardrobe in chapter seven. If you are at a restaurant/bar, I am a big proponent of sitting at the bar. The bar is a bit more relaxed, a little easier to flirt, touch (if the vibe is right), etc. Table seating can be a bit formal, but fine if that's your vibe! If you meet for coffee and you get there first, text her to ask if you should order her anything, or wait until she gets there to order together. I have heard so many complaints from women on coffee dates that their date is already seated with their coffee before they get there. C'mon, guys, rude! This is an opportunity from the get-go to show you are thinking about her, making things easier for her, and prioritizing her comfort/needs. For the record, I advise women the same re: coffee and getting there first. It's just polite.

If you are interested in your date, definitely flirt. Flirting! Oh, boy. Very important! If you are at all self-aware, you know if this comes easily to you or not. If not, it's ok. Remember, be yourself. If you would like some tips on flirting, here they are: Smile. Make eye contact (but do not stare!). Give light compliments. For example, "Wow, you look great!" or "Your pictures don't do you justice." Of course, only say this if you mean it. Compliments are appreciated, but don't lay it on too thick in the beginning. Flirting can also involve touching. Read the vibe. If she is also making eye contact, smiling, nodding, leaning in... these are signs that she is into you. Let her lead with physical touch. If she touches your arm playfully, for example, you can also engage in some light touching.

I'm putting this next tip here in the context of flirting, but it is much more important than just flirting. *Listen*. I'll say it again. *Listennnnn*. Listening first and foremost involves not talking yourself. Another opportunity for reflection here, sorry to be a wet blanket. Did your wife complain that you didn't listen to her? Did she say she just wants to "be heard"? I hear that a lot in sessions. This can mean a few different things, but at its most basic level, it means literally are you listening? Are you understanding what is important to her? Start now, on your first date. Pay attention. Act as if the world stops when the person whom you are interested in is speaking. Put your phone down! An aside, both people should be putting the phone down way more in relationships and listening to their partner. Remember things she says. Ask questions (more in a minute on what to talk about on a first date). For a first date, light convo is okay. Serious conversation is not the worst, but don't get too heavy on a first date. I know this is a fine line; you'll feel it out with practice. I've had friends and clients get asked incredibly personal questions very quickly; for example, if anyone close to them has ever died tragically or if anyone in their family struggles with addiction on a first date. Even for people who loathe small talk, this is likely too much. With time, you will share more personal information about yourself and learn more about the other person. Remember, a first date is just to see if you want to see this person for a second date! That's all it is. You don't have to "know" anything after a first date, except if you want to see the person again.

What do you talk about?? What do you not talk about?? I do think it is important to talk about the "taboo" subjects early on. For example, religion, politics, sex, etc. This does not necessarily mean on the first date, but if these things are important to you, you should find out if you align on them pretty early. Depending how you met, however, you probably at least know the basics. These issues are generally important to most people, so it makes sense to see if you align on them, though I do encourage challenging what you've thought might be a good fit in the past. Remember that annoying therapy suggestion?? Here it is again. Really think through WHY some of these things are important to you. Not that they shouldn't be, but at least think about the why.

There is a ton of advice on the internet about how to act on a first date. The "right" way to act is to be yourself. Now, because you are reading this book and thus I must assume that you are interested in introspection, self-growth, and development, I am providing some suggestions for talking points and behaviors while dating. If these feel very antithetical to who you are, that's okay! Be yourself. Remember, there is a lid for every pot. Here are some general, basic questions that can serve as jumping off points for other topics. Before getting into these, I just want to say that one of the most important things on a date (in addition to the all-important authenticity thing) is the balance between asking about the other person and sharing about yourself. You can google and find hundreds of first date questions, but here are some that have been helpful to my clients. These might seem generic, but hey, you are getting to know someone! Also, if you've talked before then you likely know some of these already, but make sure you know this basic information at the end of a first date:

- How was your day/weekend (this is maybe the best first date question)?

- What did you do (this gives some good jumping off points)?

- Where are you from (I mean, duh)?

- Who raised you?

- Where is your family now?

- Do you have any siblings?

- How do you spend your days?

- What do your weekends look like?

- What do you like to do outside of work?

- What is your ideal vacation?

- What kinds of foods do you like/not like?

- How close are you with your friends?

- What are your kids like (if applicable)?

- Do you like what you do for work?

- How long have you been in the area? What do you like/not like about it?

- Are you reading anything good? Watching anything good?

Okay, I know these seem a little interview-ey and not that cool, but this stuff is important to get to know someone! There are certainly other ways of getting to know people that I will also discuss, but the above list is just a jumping-off point. I've had clients count the number of questions men have asked them on dates, and if they have to do this, it's obviously very low. This indicates that you don't really want to get to know them. So, show interest! The truth is, if the conversation doesn't easily flow, this is not a great sign. It shows a lack of chemistry in that way, which is of course important. So it really shouldn't feel like an interview; the above questions are just places to start. There should also, of course, be laughter and levity on a first date!

When I google first date questions, I find things like:

- What do you think is important for a healthy relationship?

- What are you looking for in a partner?

- Are you often the one making plans in relationships?

- What is your love language?

- How do you handle conflict?

- What is something in past relationships you needed to work on?

Listen, these are all important things to know about someone, and I do think it is important not to shy away if they come up naturally on a first date. However, you cannot force these deeper questions too soon, and they often come off as though you are at a job interview and someone is looking for the right answer. No one wants to be put on the spot. If the relationship progresses, these things will all come to light (more on this in a later chapter), whether it is directly or by behavioral observations. For now, on a first date, the biggest thing to assess is do you actually like the person? Do you vibe/click? Are you attracted (huge)? Are they interesting? Do you want to see them again?

PAYING (AND OTHER CHIVALROUS BEHAVIOR)

Who should pay?? All-important topic. People have very strong opinions about this that run the gamut, and I have read many stories about this in the social media group mentioned in the previous chapter. Here are a few nuggets:

ONE POST (PLUS COMMENTS)

Original Post:

"Any red flags on John [picture posted under this]?? Went on a date with him and he didn't offer to pay for beer. I usually offer to split, but when they ask me to go on a date I'd expect them to at least offer to pay."

Comments:

"Just no. Always pay for yourself on a first date; this isn't 1950."

"If he can't pay for a single beer, he won't be able to provide a plate of food. Next."

"I just threw up a little. BOY BYE!"

ANOTHER

Original post:

"Hello ladies! Looking for opinions on paying for dates. For the first date, do you expect the guy to pay, you all split, or will you pick up the check?"

Comments:

"I always go in with the expectation to pay myself. I don't eat/drink anything I can't pay for. Most of the first dates I've been on, they've paid."

"Don't pay, ever. I don't even bring my wallet."

"If they don't pay, how will they take care of you?"

"If you feel no connection, you should offer to split."

"If he is a real gentleman, he will pay and not let you pay for anything."

"I always offer and I'd go out with him again if he took me up on it. I'm looking for an equal partnership and so I would never expect a man to pay for me. I think that's an outdated concept.

But if you are looking for something more traditional, your answer may be different."

"The man needs to pay. It can be coffee. It does not need to be expensive."

"If a guy asks to split it, I will not go on a second date regardless of if I am interested. I prefer someone with more traditional values so asking women to split is an indication we are not looking for the same dynamic."

ONE MORE

Original Post:

"When is the expected norm for women to start splitting the bill or take turns paying in full in early dating? I am more traditional and I think it's important to make the gesture/offer to split but I feel it's so nice when a man covers the big expenses during the courtship phase. The provider energy is very attractive to a traditional woman."

(A few) Comments:

"I don't split the bill on dates, and I don't offer. I sometimes will buy items at the grocery store for us, but even then I don't offer much. I did, however, pay for his birthday dinner lol."

"If the energy is attractive, why even offer? Want what you want and act like it."

"I split the bill from the jump so there's zero expectation or thoughts that I'm a gold digger. Courtship goes both ways."

"There is no right way; you have to communicate your personal preference."

Okay. This is what I really think about paying. And this is not PC, but I'm here to help, not be entirely PC! If YOU invite HER out, you need to pay. I mean, c'mon. Would you have dinner guests and ask them to reimburse you for ingredients? I hope not. In addition to the caveat of you asking her out, the other important assumption for our purposes is that you like her and want to see her again. If you don't, whatever, it doesn't matter. It's still a nice thing to do but matters much less of course.

Aside from common courtesy, here are the reasons why you should pay (and not take her up on it if she offers to split it, which truthfully, she shouldn't do either IF she likes you): It shows her that you value her time and company, that you like her, and that she is worth it! Don't you want to signal that she is worth the cost of drinks or dinner or COFFEE? It is NOT about the money. This is about attentiveness, caretaking, anticipating needs, making things easier for her, and the like. Some women offer to split it. This could mean a few things. It could mean she isn't into you, or it could be people-pleasing tendencies, a sign of low self-worth, or OF COURSE she might have an approach like some of the comments above in the social media group. There are definitely women who see men paying on a first date as a sign he does not want an equal partnership, and it is important for them to signal via payment they do see a partnership as equal. Also fine! Respect her preference, of course. If it aligns with yours, this is a good sign. I've had clients who have been on very "meh" dates and insisted on paying just to leave. So, if a woman is insistent on paying, don't fight it, but if you do like her, try to handle it first. I've had male clients complain that they waste money on dates when they don't like someone. Sometimes, paying for dates and not seeing her again is just how it goes! Think of it this way: Many women put a lot more time, energy, and money into getting ready for a date (wardrobe, hair, makeup, nails, etc.), and that is not cheap. Like I said before, there is always the risk of "wasted time" in dating, but I always tell my clients there is always a lesson to be learned, no matter what, so it's never a waste of time. Dating, especially post-divorce, is all about learning about yourself and what is a good fit for you.

Back to the tab. A quick note... I am speaking about the majority of straight men and women who are dating post-divorce, so we're talking at least 30s and older. I am not talking about a generation where the culture is different, which might be the case with younger folks. For my audience, a man paying for a first date does not mean an unequal relationship, as it might mean for younger people (i.e. gen z-ers, who are probably not reading this).

Most women, and probably the majority of the women you will be and want to be dating, will want to be taken care of IN THAT WAY. I am not talking about women who want sugardaddys. I literally do not personally know one such woman though I hear they exist (there are websites for them). I am talking about women who want men who are attentive, anticipate what they want/need, and do the best they can to address them. Men who make them feel safe, comfortable, secure, and AT EASE. Paying for a first date signals all those things. It says, *"I got you," "I want things to be easy for you,"* and *"don't worry about it."* Women who value themselves will want to receive that message, because they are confident they are worth it. This is probably the type of woman you want to be dating. The confident, self-assured woman who knows she is worth the cost of a first date!

One last reason to pay. This is the most practical one. It shows that you CAN. I am all for women making as much/more money than their partners, but, of course, everyone wants someone who can literally cover the cost of a meal. Again, this is not an indicator she wants you to financially support her. There might be other clues for that (remember the red flags for it online), but wanting you to pay for a first date is not that. Paying on a first date is also a turn-on! For all the above reasons. Moving forward in a relationship, this can—and should—be discussed! Attitudes about money/spending is an important area for compatibility, and this is a good way to gauge it early on. It can be discussed on a first date too, but remember that a first date is just that.

Okay, first date over. Congrats! Hopefully, at least you had some interesting conversation or found a new fun spot.

Please offer to walk her to her car or metro or whatever, or wait with her for a car. You can also offer to walk or drive her home if you are close by. Actually, the best way to handle this is to say something like, "I'd love to walk/drive you home, but I understand if you don't want me to know where you live on a first date." This is chivalrous but also conveys understanding of what dating is like for her. Then, let her decide. Many women won't want you knowing where she lives on a first date, unless she's inviting you there (also more on that in the next chapter). Accept a "no" if she declines any of the above offers please. Then, please check to see if she got home okay (if you didn't walk or drive her, obviously).

On this note! I recently read a study conducted by Tinder and what a perfect place to share the results! Tinder recently (May 2024) conducted a survey of 8,000 participants (ages 18-34, so I understand this might be slightly outside the demographic here, but it is still interesting). The takeaway from the study, called "The Green Flag" study, was that both men and women assume so much about the opposite sex that they miss out on a lot of opportunities. It discussed what men and women are looking for in terms of romantic relationships or casual flings, but the biggest takeaway for YOU, my dear readers, on the topic of first dates, is the data on what women perceive to be chivalrous these days.

According to this study, the top three chivalrous behaviors are: checking to make sure your date got home okay (59%), putting away your phone on dates (55%), and giving sincere compliments (50%). In contrast, men think that the most important chivalrous behaviors for women to receive are paying the check and being on time. This is so interesting, right?

What is it about those top three behaviors that women like? It is attention and caretaking. Making sure they got home okay is a signal you will watch out for their safety. Putting the phone down means your attention is on them, you are actually focused, interested, and paying attention. Giving SINCERE compliments means you can recognize the woman sitting in front of you and put words to it! So important (see section on "words of affirmation").

I wrote a whole thing above about paying on the first date, and I generally stand by this, however, it is not surprising to me that it does not rate higher than the behaviors I just mentioned. Women can pay for their meals; there are more important things. And being on time, c'mon. The bar is low. Don't celebrate the low bar. Be the one who raises it!

KISSING

A note on kissing. Should you kiss her? Sure, if you want to and sense that she does too. I hear a lot of hesitations from my male clients about being too forward/too aggressive regarding kissing and expressing interest in kissing, and I hear you. Most women you are dating want a confident guy on the dominant side in this domain.

So, remember these very important words: "I'd really like to kiss you." This conveys a few important things: One, you are attracted to her (good for this to be reinforced); two, you are confident enough to make a move; and three, you ARE in fact waiting/asking for consent, but you are just doing it in an assertive way. And then, you wait for consent. This could be verbal, or it could be in the form of facial expressions/body language (for example, head nodding, eye contact, smiling, physically leaning in).

Another gem from me to you regarding kissing: some women like it when you *gently* hold their face and neck (yes, kind of like in the movies). Put your thumbs on their cheekbones and stroke gently. In terms of actual kissing, please do not use too much tongue. Tongue is there to aid but in a gentle way. As you get to know each other better (and communicate about what you like), you can be a bit more playful like nibbling her lip or tugging her hair.

More on kissing (and other fun things) in the next chapter.

COMMUNICATION AFTER

If you don't want to see her again:

If this is the case, you don't have to do anything. It is not "ghosting" if neither of you follow up after a date. It is just a sign of mutual disinterest. If she is reaching out and wanting to go out again, or even texting/calling and you get the sense that she wants to see you again, you can/should say something like, "Hey, I had a nice time getting to know you, but I just don't feel the romantic connection I am looking for. Best of luck!" This is direct, straightforward, and honest without giving too much unnecessary information that would hurt someone's feelings. That is the goal: enough to get the point across, but you don't have to give details. It is also much better than not responding at all.

Women appreciate directness, maturity, and honesty. Please do not try to protect her feelings by avoiding her. This does not do her any favors—she can handle it, gentleman. More on this topic in the "Breaking Up" chapter still to come.

If you want to see her again:

Let her know! Schedule the next date later that night or the next day. Do not leave her wondering if you want to see her again. Do not play games; there is no reason to wait on this. I will say, unless you are 100000% sure she wants to see you again, wait until after the date to ask her out again via text (as opposed to in person on date one).

You could also end the date with, "I'd love to see you again. I'll text you to set something up!" This takes the pressure off the moment, lets her know you are interested, and sets expectations. Then, follow up. Do not say that if you aren't interested! You can just end the date with, "It was so nice to meet you. Get home safe!". I still think it is polite to make sure she got home okay, but that does not signal intent for a second date. Just try your best to avoid mixed messages.

Texting, in the early days of dating, should be limited to making plans and the occasional checking in. Texting too much too soon creates a sense of connection that might not play out IRL. This could also be a sign of anxious attachment. Secure people want to date secure people, who have enough going on they do not constantly text.

On the other hand, you do want her to know you are interested in her, so you can (and should) check in in between dates, just don't text too much. A short exchange daily or every other day is fine in the beginning, and then can increase as you get to know each other more and integrate more into each other's lives (if you do).

TL;DR

- Pick a place for a first date that is easy and low-pressure, and you can actually talk. Offer to go to an area close to her.

- Flirt. Listen. Put the phone down. Ask questions. Make appropriate eye contact. Give sincere and light compliments.

- Pick up the tab if you like her, but don't insist if she insists.

- Chivalry is still important. Checking if she got home okay and putting the phone down are important ways to be chivalrous; it is not all related to picking up the check.

- Make a move to kiss her IF there are signs she is into it.
- Follow-up quickly and be direct if you want to see her again.

HOMEWORK

- ☐ If you are chatting with anyone on an app, ask them out!
- ☐ Make a list of good first date places in your city/town.
- ☐ Introspect about your first date behavior thus far. What have you noticed? What is working? What isn't?

CHAPTER 10

ORAL SEX IS NOT FOREPLAY

What No One Tells You About Sex and What it is Really About

"I didn't wanna fake it again, so I just forgot to return his last call." —MIRANDA

"You broke up with an ophthalmologist over that?" —CHARLOTTE

"Orgasm, major thing in a relationship?" —MIRANDA

"But not the only thing. Orgasms don't send you Valentine's cards and don't hold your hand in a sad movie." —CHARLOTTE

"You're seriously advocating faking?" —MIRANDA

"No, but if you really like the guy, what's one little moment of 'ooh and ahhh' versus spending the whole night in bed alone?" —CHARLOTTE

"These are my options!?" —MIRANDA

"Who's to say that one moment is any more important than when he gets up and pours you a cup of coffee in the morning?" —CHARLOTTE

*"I'll take an orgasm over a cup of French
drip Colombian any day."* —MIRANDA

"For me, it's a toss-up." —CARRIE

*"While women are certainly no strangers to faking
it ... we've faked our hair color, cup size, hell, we've
even faked fur. I couldn't help but wonder, has fear of
being alone suddenly raised the bar on faking? Are
we faking more than orgasms? Are we faking entire
relationships? Is it better to fake it than be alone?"*
—CARRIE'S VOICEOVER, AFTER THE CONVERSATION ABOVE

There are so many good quotes that could have opened this chapter (of course, much of the show is about sex!), but I chose this one because the takeaway is SO important! No, of course it is not better to fake it than be alone! In the scene above, Miranda is talking about how she "forgot" to return "Josh the Ophthalmologist'"'s call because he didn't know how to get her off. The episode continues on to depict Miranda trying to teach him how to get her off, him not getting it, her faking it again, and not calling him back again.

SEX IS NOT "JUST" SEX

Finally, we get to the all-important sex chapter(s)! This chapter is about sex and several important things that come along with it (no pun intended). I will be talking (briefly; there are a million resources about all this, check the back for recommendations) about sexual desire, foreplay, sexual compatibility, and orgasms. The goal is twofold: one, to help you understand what might have happened in your marriage and previous relationships regarding your sex life, and two, so you understand all this important stuff for the future! Statistically speaking, odds are good you will get married again, and I want to arm you with the knowledge you likely didn't have before you got married. I would also venture your sexual confidence is not all that high (unless by the time you are reading this you have gotten some of that back, which is great! Still read on), and this might help to give some perspective on your past and engender some optimism about the future.

The first thing to note about sex is: Sex is never just about sex. Ever. EVER. Even if it is a one-night stand (ONS), it is about more than that. Although, let's be honest here, it IS ALSO about the physical act, because sex and orgasms feel pretty good! Well, if you're doing it right! Lots of yummy hormones are released. Physical touch also increases immunity and lowers stress. It is okay to want something that feels good, like ice cream. And blow jobs. Sex is ALSO about intimacy, connection, communication, vulnerability, romance, exploration, play, feeling close and connected, getting your needs met, understanding someone else's needs, feeling sexy and desired, novelty, and excitement, to name a few things. I hear this from both men and women, especially if your love language is physical touch (more on this in a later chapter)! Our definition of "sex" continues to be pretty limited and heteronormative, and I challenge you to expand your definition of sex from what is likely focused on penis in vulva penetration, and open your mind to all kinds of sexual acts falling under the umbrella of sex.

DESIRE AND FOREPLAY

Good place to start! Before we jump into "when can I fuck this new girl I'm dating?" (humor me that you would listen anyway), it's important to discuss some basics. I am devoting an entire section to the incredibly important topic of foreplay. Please note that it is not under the category of sex. Here's the thing about foreplay. It is everything; this cannot be overstated. It is not optional. It should make up the majority of your sexual encounter. Especially for women, though for men too (even though society might have you think otherwise). Although this is a section about dating and when you first start being sexual with someone, foreplay is especially important in long-term monogamy, because most women have responsive desire. It is important that you understand this concept even at the beginning of dating!

RESPONSIVE AND SPONTANEOUS DESIRE

This is as good a place as any to stop and discuss responsive and spontaneous desire. This will be a very brief overview, and if you want a more in-depth discussion, there are a lot of books on the subject (the main one being *Come as You Are* by Emily Negoski). To break it down in broad strokes, most men (and women in the honeymoon stages of a relationship) have spontaneous desire, which means that they think about sex many (sometimes many, many, many) times per day and are very easily aroused by things like: seeing an attractive person, remembering a sexy time, a dream, thinking about a fantasy, their wife bending over, etc. It's basically like what porn would have you think about arousal: that people are just ready to go at any time. Their arousal is spontaneous. This is often part of the rush of hormones of the early relationship stage ("New Relationship Energy," more on that later too).

In contrast, responsive desire is seen more often in women in long-term monogamous relationships, where arousal takes warming up. This will sound dramatic, but please understand that women in long-term monogamous relationships (especially with kids and jobs and lots on their plate) think about sex with their long-term partners as much as you think about... sending holiday cards to your in-laws, or your kid's favorite board game. Truly, sex is not on their mind much of the day (if at all, depending on what is going on in their lives). The caveat to this—and the time when she might feel spontaneous desire—is when she is ovulating. So, a few days a month she might have been more receptive to sex, touching, she might have been nicer in general, even initiated sex, etc. This is evolution! Biology! This is a good reason to track your partner's cycle, so you can be in tune with her mood, irritability, sex drive, etc.

Anyway.

The rest of the time, in long-term monogamy, she likely has responsive desire. This does NOT mean that she doesn't like sex, although it is also possible that she truly is not a sexual person and/or you were sexually incompatible (more later on that). Responsive desire is just the opposite of spontaneous desire: sexual activity can begin, then arousal will follow, THEN desire will happen in RESPONSE to the arousal, not the other way around as is the case with spontaneous desire. Women with responsive desire are not ready to have sex immediately. They need to be aroused FIRST, before actually wanting sex. Meaning sexual activity needs to start before she is aroused. Here is an analogy. Her being aroused immediately would be the equivalent of you being in a work meeting and your wife coming up to you and asking you to write her a love letter immediately RIGHT NOW. You are not in the headspace for this. Same thing with responsive desire. Cue the need for a) relaxation, and b) foreplay. If women are stressed and anxious, they will not be able to get in the headspace of being aroused. Emily

Negoski discusses the "brakes" and the "gas" of female sexual desire, and women have a lot more brakes than men do. If you remember your ex-wife (or another long term partner) not wanting to have sex at night because the kids might walk in, or she can't focus because she is thinking about her to-do list, these are the "brakes," and the things that get in the way of relaxation. She was too tense for sex—the brakes are on. The doors need to be locked, she needs to feel physically relaxed, etc. The brakes need to be off, AND the gas needs to be on. Meaning, she needs to not be stressed at that moment, AND she needs to be turned on. An aside—this is where massage is a great tool to use moving forward. Massage should be used to relax your partner, NOT to "get them" to have sex, but in general if they are relaxed, they will be much more likely to want to. Make sense? Relaxation and foreplay are imperative for responsive desire. And speaking her love language, which is often akin to removing the brakes. I have a whole chapter on love languages coming up. And, perhaps most important... making sure the sex is great and worth the "trouble" to activate responsive desire. Often, when I talk to my female clients about their sex lives (particularly within monogamy), they will reveal that the sex they are having isn't great. So, of course, they are not motivated to have it! Foreplay is an essential part of great sex.

A lot of people don't know that women's sex drives wane within long-term monogamy (ugh, the sex ed in this country is abysmal), and the lack of knowledge around this leads to a lot of problems in relationships! This is really important to understand! It is biology and happens without fail after the honeymoon period. Men take things personally (thinking your wife isn't attracted to you, for example) and often feel very hurt and misunderstood when they are rejected for sex. It is especially confusing when women get turned on by characters in shows or movies or someone IRL. This is also evolution! A new partner, or the idea of one, might engender spontaneous desire for her. But in long-term monogamy, it is different. Not *bad*, just different! Often, a man's solution to this is to start working out like crazy or otherwise focus on physical aspects in the hope that their wives will be attracted to them again. This is not the solution, friends, because lack of attraction is (typically, in healthy relationships), not what is happening here. While it is true that most women want men who take care of themselves, this is not the key to increasing sexual desire, and is most definitely not why your marriage did not work out. Men also think that women sometimes pull a "bait and switch" on them because they were into sex in the beginning and are not anymore. This is biology, not a bait and switch. There are things you probably did early on in the relationship that you aren't doing anymore either. This is due to NRE waning, not a bait and switch. It is essential that if you remarry, that you not only marry someone who is sexually compatible, but that you understand responsive and spontaneous desire. Her sex drive will inevitably decrease, but at least you can have a better understanding of it. If you are hoping to activate your partner's responsive desire, make sure she is nice and relaxed and feels connected to you. This often relates to acts of service or another love language, which is covered in a later chapter.

FOREPLAY: WHAT IT ISN'T

So, what is foreplay? Let me start by saying what it is NOT. You very well-meaning men who are focused on their partner's pleasure, please read carefully. Truly, if you take not a single other thing from this book, please take this: foreplay is NOT going down on a woman. This. Is. Sex. Need to hear it again? Oral sex is sex, not foreplay. DrPsychMom has an entire podcast on this, go listen if you are curious. What does this mean in the context of the above paragraph on responsive desire?? It means that when you (again, very nicely and well-meaning, I'm sure) offer to go down on her to do something nice for her, to get her in the mood, to get her off, you are jumping to something she is not ready for! It would truly be like just sticking your dick inside her with zero warming up. Or, for a different analogy: It would be like if your partner suddenly out of nowhere while you were doing the dishes asked you to stop and immediately tell her the ten things you love about her and why you chose her. I know this falls into a trope about women liking romance and men liking sex but a.) this is often what I see, and b.) this does not mean that men don't like romantic words of affirmation and women don't like sex; my point is simply that it's about how to get in the headspace for it. If you were having a romantic evening, talking, connecting, flirting, and THEN she wanted you to tell her why she is the best, that would be very different than, "Hey honey, tell me RIGHT NOW why you love me," completely out of nowhere.

Note that the analogy is not her offering to give you a random blowjob, because I'm guessing you would be into that! Because you have spontaneous desire, so you will get aroused (easily!) by the thought of a blowjob, whereas women with responsive desire will look at you like you've just suggested that she get up out of bed and do a triathlon when you suggest going down on her out of nowhere. One last thing and then I've probably harped on this enough: This does not mean she does not like oral sex. In the context of other sexual activity and being aroused (and if she is a sexual person), she likes it! Just not out of nowhere. Many of my male clients tell me their female partners don't like receiving oral, and this is often the reason. That's actually not true, she's just not ready (i.e. not turned on). She should already be wet by the time you go down on her, and just in general do anything involving her genitals. So really, foreplay does not involve genital stimulation of any kind (on her!). That is SEX. But also, if she truly doesn't like receiving oral, she might not like how you do it.

While we are on the topic, a word on oral sex

It is still a good thing to do, so I'll just give some tips for it. You can—and should!—use the leadup to oral as a form of foreplay. You can tease her by kissing/licking her inner thigh, around her genitals, etc. You can nibble on her underwear. Prolong this. When you get to the good stuff and are actually going down on her, give her compliments (tell her how much you like doing it, tell her she tastes good), use your fingers to penetrate as well. Keep a steady rhythm with both your tongue and your hands; don't switch it up too much. Ask her if she likes the pressure. Women typically need consistent rhythm/pressure to orgasm (this goes for penetration as well), NOT what you may see in porn where she is constantly flipped around. If she tells you not to stop, do NOT stop. She may or may not orgasm from oral—something to find out about! More on orgasms later. But, if she is a sexual person, she will likely still like it when it is not part of foreplay and instead as part of sex once she is aroused. You can/should go back to going down on her as a break from penetrative sex as well. Good to mix it up! Just start to think about oral sex in the bucket of sex, not foreplay, so do it accordingly. Same with manual stimulation.

FOREPLAY: WHAT IT IS

So, what IS foreplay?? Everything else! The good stuff. The stuff you see teenagers do in coming-of-age movies. Kissing (various places, but not genitals, but breasts are okay, yes!), touching, caressing her face and body, massage, compliments, eye contact, talking (many women like dirty talk. More on that in a minute), dry humping (remember that??). Teasing is also pretty arousing for a lot of women. Teasing might involve telling her what you are going to do, but not doing it. Withholding in a playful way. Or stopping and starting. For example, getting close to her genitals but not touching them, or touching lightly over her clothes. It could involve pulling away while kissing and coming back. But keep eye contact and connection if doing this. Here is the other CRUCIAL thing about foreplay: it starts from the moment you meet/connect. It starts in the morning (i.e. bringing her coffee), at night (i.e. asking about her day, following up on something she has mentioned before), it's all throughout the day. It is how you treat her in general. Does she feel safe, does she trust you, does she feel like you are prioritizing her and making her feel special? These are either major turn-ONs, or major turn-OFFs. So, foreplay is most certainly not limited to the bedroom.

Foreplay is also compliments, as these are often major turn-ons for women, which is why it can happen all throughout the day! I discuss words of affirmation in a later chapter, but in general an arousing compliment involves eye contact, sincerity, and in this context of foreplay, telling her things like: "I want you," "you are so [gorgeous, sexy, etc.]," "I've thought about this all day," or "I can't get you out of my head." A lot of times what foreplay is really about is the focus and attention on her (a major turn-on)—all the above conveys that.

Back to kissing

This is super important for most women (and men, I know you like it too!), and it is the thing that wanes in long-term monogamy, which is often a reason women are not turned on/ready for sex. There might be several reasons for this waning. One, you might not like the way your partner kisses, but you were never given the tools to be able to talk about it, so you just avoid it. This goes for all communication around sex—it is not easy! More on that in a bit. Another reason kissing can wane is poor hygiene (refer back to my earlier chapter on grooming/hygiene). Lastly, in relation to foreplay, if anyone has ever told you to stop kissing and just get to the sex, this is a clear indicator that they were not aroused enough to have sex. Husbands will tell me in session that they are just obliging their wives if they tell them to hurry up (and at that point they often take whatever sex they are "allowed" to have, which is also not a good situation!). This is actually when you slow down and tease and actually turn her on, to the point where she actually wants more.

Kissing is not pecking. Kissing involves deep kisses and tongue (but not TOO much). Discuss early on how you and your partner like to be kissed, and take/give feedback. If you don't have the kissing down, there are major problems to come. The following goes for essentially any sexual act, but kissing as well: please do not let your ego get in the way of good kissing/foreplay/oral sex/sex. Talk about what you like. Few people are taught (well) how to do this, so, you have to learn from experience and trial and error. Plus, everyone is different and likes different things! Please take the time and effort to learn your partner (I have specific questions listed in a few sections). Pro tip: talk about these things outside of a sexual setting. It is often too vulnerable/awkward to discuss what you like/what does or does not feel good when you are naked and in bed. Talk about it outside of the bedroom! There are many prompts, games, question cards, etc. out there now (a few listed in the back of the book!) that can help prompt these conversations that I know are awkward (because again, we aren't taught).

SEXUAL COMPATIBILITY

Oh, how important. If you and your wife were not sexually compatible and you convinced yourself there are more important things in a relationship, pay attention here. If you yourself are not a sexual person, no judgment. But please do not dismiss this need if you are. Like I mentioned before, sex is about so much more than just sex. More on physical touch as a love language in a later chapter, so here I will focus on sexual desires and compatibility.

An additional thought on sexual compatibility: it can be an evolving thing. People often think of it as very black-and-white, like either you are compatible or not. But you can learn more things about each other, desires change, curiosity changes, so compatibility can also grow and be fluid. That said, if it IS very clear you are not compatible from the jump and sex is important to you, do not proceed.

WHAT ARE YOU INTO? EROTIC BLUEPRINTS

Wherever you are in your post-divorce journey, you may or may not have had some time to explore your sexuality a bit more. Perhaps you had a lot of partners before your wife, or perhaps not. Either way, you likely have a good sense of what turns you on, at least in terms of fantasies, though you might not have experienced all the things you are curious about.

Erotic blueprints are one tool (there are many ways to figure out what you are into) that can be used to help you (and future/current partners) figure out what turns you on! I'll give an overview of the types, but of course feel free to google and take a quiz yourself! You might not even need a quiz to know what turns you on. Here are the types:

SENSUAL TYPE: This is a person who is turned on by the senses, so taste, touch, smell, etc. They are turned on by the setting in particular, so a beautiful setting is helpful if you are this type. This person might be able to orgasm from non-genital stimulation.

ENERGETIC TYPE: This person gets turned on by... yes, energy. So, things like anticipation, longing, yearning, teasing. This person is often highly sensitive, so it doesn't take much.

SEXUAL TYPE: This person is turned on by what we typically think of when we think about sex in today's culture. For example, nudes, thoughts about penetration, genitals, orgasm, etc.

KINKY TYPE: This person is turned on by more taboo things. Examples of kink can include toys, bondage, role-play, power dynamics, impact play, BDSM. Truly this could take up a whole chapter and many books, but you get the idea for now. If you are curious about kink, see the list of resources in the back of the book.

SHAPESHIFTER TYPE: This one is of course turned on by all of it, just depends on the mood! They are often turned on by whatever turns on their partner as well.

So, think about your erotic blueprint! Think about your ex's too. This might be more challenging. I'm sure she has one ("frigidity" is not an erotic blueprint). Was this an incompatibility? Were you more kinky while your wife was more sensual? Consider this moving forward with new partners. Of course, it is easier when they match (as is the case with most things, like a carnivore dating a vegan. Doable but much harder).

I've had many couples in couple's therapy take this quiz and discover they have different erotic blueprints. This is okay; you just need to understand them! Everyone has different preferences/turn-ons. Open-mindedness is key, no matter what. Don't yuck someone's yum.

ORGASMS

This highlights the definite importance of orgasming during sexual activity! Like I mentioned previously, female orgasms are generally not like they are in porn, meaning they do not happen one after the other with relative ease. On one hand, it is not ONLY about the orgasm. I often hear from women clients that they orgasm but the sex is not great. On the other hand, they are not unimportant.

Sex is definitely much more than orgasm, but it is also pretty frustrating not to orgasm. I'm sure you can relate to this frustration! So, lots more to sex than orgasm, but also, don't neglect it. Especially given responsive desire and how it takes effort on the part of women to be willing to get in the headspace to have sex, it can be even more frustrating. It would be like spending a lot of time cooking a meal that isn't delicious.

Women also generally like it when their male partner orgasms. It is a turn on. This is often why it does not go without saying that "she comes first." Sometimes, a woman will get turned on when a man comes and that arousal can eventually lead to her orgasm.

Another important note: just because you come does not mean a sexual encounter is over. Sometimes women are close or are generally enjoying themselves, and when a man orgasms and just ends the encounter, it can be frustrating. Check in with her after and express eagerness to continue with your mouth, hands, or a toy to get her off. Before you claim fatigue, remember the days in your 20s when you would take three buses and trains in order to hook up and then back home again after you came? Channel that 20-something energy and make sure the encounter doesn't end with your orgasm if she hasn't come yet.

Please don't focus TOO much on the orgasm to the point where it is annoying (please stop asking "are you gonna cum?"). This is obviously another place where feedback is really important! Ask her what she likes OUTSIDE of a sexual scenario; this takes the pressure off. Be super open and not judgmental.

Here are some specific questions you can ask: What type of manual stimulation does she like? How many fingers? Ask what type of pressure she likes, the intensity of touching, the pace, etc. Same with oral stimulation. Ask how much pressure she likes and what she likes you to do with your mouth. Of course this all needs to be in the context of a conversation you are having; don't ask these questions out of left field.

I mentioned before that women generally need consistent rhythm and pressure to orgasm. For women, it takes about 10-15 minutes of this consistency to orgasm. Also, please keep in mind that most women (70%) do not orgasm from penetration alone; they need clitoral stimulation. Pretend it's a science experiment and you are looking at it through a lens of curiosity. She might not know the answers to these (this is also a clue about how sexual a person she might be), so don't push it, but make sure she knows you want to hear what feels good for her.

Women are also not taught how to figure out what feels good and they may not know! Give it some time. They may also feel self-conscious about expressing what feels good and what they want. You can model this by being emotionally vulnerable in situations other than sex. This is all related to orgasm. If women can relax and feel comfortable and safe with you, it will be easier to figure out what they like (if they don't know), and they will be much more open about communicating it to you.

For women, orgasms are a skill that needs to be learned. It is not as simple as "relax," and "feel connected." No way. They need to know what makes them feel good. It's like training for any skill. Be eager to know what they know about their bodies, but don't push.

A note on vibrators

There are some women who essentially rely on vibrators to orgasm. Your role in a sexual scenario is to be non-judgmental so she feels comfortable telling you what she is into, as discussed. If she needs a vibrator to orgasm, no big deal! This is not a personal shortcoming on your part. Some women have basically conditioned themselves to need one. Just let her know you are supportive of her pleasure, regardless of what that consists of. Be willing and happy to lend a... whatever it is that will get her there (but again, don't make it all about that; this puts too much pressure on it).

Ideally, you would both be able to get each other off without added assistance, but this also takes time. Follow her lead on this: if she wants to orgasm without a vibrator, cool. If not, also okay. However, if it really does bother you, talk to her about it. It's understandable if you want to make her come without relying on a device, this is very intimate and connected. Don't let it be an ego thing, though. Make it about connection and intimacy, and just continue to be a safe space in lots of different ways. Again, it's all related.

Faking it

We hear about women faking orgasms, but we hear less about men doing it. I think probably women and men fake orgasms for similar reasons. It can be one of a few things: it is just not going to happen; they want to end the sexual encounter; they do not know how to tell their partner what they want and they don't want to hurt their feelings if it isn't working for them. These are all understandable, but please don't ever fake an orgasm, or anything sexual that you don't like. That doesn't mean don't do things for your partner that you yourself are not super into, it means don't FAKE things.

Again, most of us are not taught to talk openly about sex so it can be very difficult to do so, and can feel very awkward. But it is worth it! Getting to know your partner and vice versa is truly erotic, and is imperative for a great sex life.

As I've discussed (and will continue to), when someone is unfulfilled in an important area, it is very problematic. Not being open about what you like is a major example of this, and can lead to a profound lack of fulfillment. Communicate about what feels good and does not feel good. If you fake it (orgasms or anything that you are faking), you are not teaching your partner what you like, and you are reinforcing something you don't like or that isn't working, leading to unsatisfying at best, or bad, at worst sex! You aren't protecting them by faking orgasms; they aren't fragile. A well-adjusted, confident person will want to know what you want.

I've seen couples in my practice where the woman has been faking it for years. It's very difficult to come back from that, so definitely do not start out that way. No faking, and no giving HER reasons to do so (i.e. by being closed-minded, judgmental, defensive, etc.)!

TL;DR:

- Sex is never just sex. It is about intimacy, connection, vulnerability, exploration, playfulness, open-mindedness, etc.

- There are different types of desire: spontaneous and responsive.

- Most women in long term monogamous relationships have responsive desire. This is normal.

- Foreplay is essential, and does NOT involve the genitals.

- Foreplay takes place way outside the bedroom as well.

- Kissing is crucial.

- Learn how to tease and turn on, and take your time.

- Oral sex is still important. Learn what your partner likes.

- Erotic blueprints can tell you a lot about what turns you on.

- Orgasms are not the be-all-end-all, but they are not unimportant. Be open and non-judgmental.

- No faking! Anything!!!

HOMEWORK:

- ☐ Think back on your sex life with your previous partners, and how these concepts may or may not apply.

- ☐ Google "responsive desire" to learn more.

- ☐ Take an erotic blueprint quiz and think about your previous partners. Was there an issue with compatibility? Introspect on this.

CHAPTER 11

LET'S TALK ABOUT SEX (AGAIN)

What Really Matters in the Bedroom

"And even when you take all the precautions and emotionally try to protect yourself, when you climb into bed with someone, is sex ever safe?" —CARRIE

In the quote above, Carrie is referencing how Samantha was dating Tom Reymi, a "Manhattan legend" who wanted her to get tested for AIDS before they slept together. Simultaneously, she is having an affair with Mr. Big and referring to the emotional risks involved in that relationship. In this chapter, I will discuss when to have sex when you are starting to see someone, the art of initiation, dominance, and contact after sex.

WHEN TO HAVE SEX?

The short answer here is: when both people want to! There is lots of dating advice that tells women to wait to have sex. The book *The Rules* written by Ellen Fein and Sherrie Schneider in 1995 advises women to wait until women are out of the early dating phase to have sex. They also advise women to rarely return phone calls and be generally pretty aloof. In her book *Never Waste Time on the Wrong Man Again*, author Michelle Jacoby encourages women who are looking for a serious relationship not to sleep with men until they are exclusive. She encourages assuaging a prospect's concerns that a woman might not be so into sex by suggesting they tell men something along the lines of "I am a super sexual person, I'm into you, but I'm waiting for exclusivity."

Some women abide by a "three date rule." The social media group I have referenced several times is full of advice on this as well. It runs the gamut from women waiting until marriage to things like "no big deal if you fuck on the first date." Women have shared many stories about how they are married to someone they slept with right away, in addition to stories like, "I waited for months, and he still broke up with me."

Of course, the women of *Sex and the City* have strong opinions about this. Charlotte advises Carrie to not sleep with Big when she is getting ready to go on their first date. She states that, "if you are serious about a guy, you have to keep him in a holding pattern for at least five dates." Miranda agrees with not on a first date, though does not provide a magic number, and Samantha chimes in with a reality check that a guy can just as easily dump you if you have sex on the first date or the tenth. Spoiler alert: Carrie and Big fuck on the first date, although they have met each other several times before their actual "official date." They eventually, after MUCH back and forth over years, get married. This ends tragically in the reboot *And Just Like That*, but I won't spoil EVERYTHING here. The moral is: does it really matter?

The alleged wisdom behind the advice to wait is that women get more attached after sex due to the release of bonding hormones, so they are more likely to get hurt if they sleep with someone without establishing trust that they are not going to leave them (i.e. not call/text). I would argue there are lots of things that facilitate attachment that are not sex, including things like deep conversations, hand holding, kissing, texting, other new experiences that are not related to sex, etc. Men also get attached after sex, for the record. Especially good sex.

I think if sex is important to you in a relationship and you have a high sex drive, you are probably not a fit for someone who wants to wait a long time. I also think that the question of how long to wait to have sex depends on what you are looking for. If you are looking for a serious partnership, it makes sense to wait a bit and get to know each other. If you are just looking for casual fun, this doesn't really apply. However, as mentioned, please be as honest as your self-awareness allows, and if you need help developing your self-awareness, therapy can be very useful!

Also, keep in mind that it is likely that the women you are dating have been hurt in the past regarding sex. Things that I have seen include: being ghosted after sex, being pushed to have sex sooner than they wanted, receiving unwanted attention, harassment, and unfortunately, of course, sexual trauma/assault. All of that is important to be aware of and be sensitive to. Just because a woman doesn't sleep with you right away does not mean she doesn't love sex. I talk about how to tell if this is an area of compatibility shortly.

If you like someone, get to know them. If, after a little while, things don't seem to be progressing in that way, this is something to talk about. Of course, many men have also been burned. I am just hoping to build some empathy and awareness around why women who are very sexual might wait to have sex. Of course, if you are on completely different pages regarding various aspects of sex (i.e. when to have it, the type of sex you like, etc.), this could be a dealbreaker (more later on that).

SAFETY FIRST

I'm putting this early in the chapter because I just think it's so important to say up front. So bear with me for this quick throwback to fifth grade and a note on safe sex. PLEASE have a conversation about safe sex and birth control before you have penetrative sex. Or, if you don't have a conversation about it, please default to condoms. Women appreciate it when men take the lead on this. It signals that their health and safety matters to them, and says the opposite when men try to fuck without them. This action assumes that women are taking the lead on birth control and that you, as a man, are not taking responsibility for it. The takeaway from the woman's perspective when this happens is "he doesn't care if something happens (i.e. needing to take plan B, pregnancy, STIs) to me."

Women are at higher risks for STIs and obviously pregnancy, and are thus significantly more vulnerable with unprotected sex. I continue to be surprised by the frequency with which this happens to my single clients and girlfriends who are sexually active. Defaulting to condoms is the ultimate act of protection, and how you can show your partner you are keeping them safe, regardless of the relationship status at this point. We are all aware that sex feels better without a condom, so this signals that you are putting her safety above your pleasure. This is true even if you have had a vasectomy. There is a lot of misinformation and stigma around STIs, and the truth is a lot of them are really not a huge deal but better to avoid!

Best case scenario is you talk about it like adults. Of course, it takes two to tango, like everything else, and she has responsibility as well, but I want to share the important female perspective here. If/when your relationship progresses, you can keep discussing sexual health and birth control and see where you both are in terms of losing the condoms.

Lastly, a woman's desire to use condoms is not in any way reflective of her being prudish or vanilla. I don't think I've encountered any woman where condoms are preferred! They are just necessary until otherwise decided.

INITIATING

Initiating sex is definitely an art. I discussed how to initiate kissing in the last chapter, so I will discuss taking it further here. This is again something that is more about principles than an exact protocol, and requires one to read the signals. I will say, you should make a move if you are into her. Women, if they like you, want to be wanted. So, if you are making out and you like each other, you can initiate more by touching her more intensely, gently pulling her closer, kissing more passionately, etc.

Also, like I mentioned regarding kissing, use your words to let her know how you feel. Refer back to that section, but I mainly mean variations on things like *"I can't get you out of my head," "I want you," "You are so beautiful,"* etc. Make sure to make eye contact while saying these things. So important.

HOWEVER, please heed the response and read the room. If she is cold/unresponsive/resistant/hesitant, do not push. Follow her lead while also letting her know you are interested. It's a balance. Ask her if you are not sure. This will always be appreciated. If you are having trouble reading if she wants to go further, ask her. Say something like, *"I'm really into you and I'd love to take it further, but I am having trouble reading your signals. What do you think?"*

Communication is always appreciated, even if it sounds awkward. It is actually more appreciated if it is awkward, because that means you care enough about how she is feeling to have an awkward conversation. This principle applies to most things in the relationship!

I would be remiss if I did not add a few "don'ts" of initiating: Do NOT just grab her when you want sex. This goes back to the importance of foreplay. Don't just grab her breasts, or her butt, when you are in the mood. She likely will experience this as juvenile and silly, and definitely not sexy.

Also, do not initiate with a joke. Don't make innuendos either. These are both immature and show a lack of confidence. Be direct and confident and sexy. You might be funny as a human, but joking around during initiation and even sex is a turn-off for most women (I'm not talking about if something funny happens; you can't take sex SO seriously). You'll never see a sexy scene in a show or a movie that starts with a silly joke.

Channel some confidence, even if you don't fully have it. Confidence is sexy. You might have lost some confidence initiating sex while you were married, so just think about this moving forward.

If you are in an ongoing relationship and struggling with initiation, the above tips are still important. You can also ask things like *"are you open to being turned on?"* as opposed to something like *"do you want to have sex?"* (@Vanessaandxander talk about this approach on their social media). Because remember, if you just outright ask her if she wants to have sex she will likely say no; because of responsive desire, she is probably not turned on at the moment.

A WORD ON DOMINANCE

Most—but not all—women like when there is a bit of dominance in the bedroom. Before I proceed with this topic, let me just be very clear: dominance does NOT mean anything non-consensual. Everyone get that? These are VERY different things. I am talking about taking charge within the context of a consensual sexual relationship.

Something like 80% of women fantasize about being dominated. If you want to hear more about this and more very interesting research on sexual fantasies in general, check out the *Sex and Psychology* podcast hosted by sociologist Dr. Justin Lehmiller.

Most of the women in my practice, my friends, and from what I have seen on the amazing anthropological "experiment" that is the social media group that I mentioned before, express similar desires. This can be especially true for women with a lot going on—women with impressive careers, kids, active social lives, etc. These women often do not want to have to make decisions or think about things, and really do fantasize about male sexual partners taking control. In fact, according to Dr. Lehmiller's podcast, a lot of women fantasize about "forced sex."

Let me just pause real quick here to clarify an incredibly important point: This does NOT mean that women WANT to be raped!! This is a fantasy, which has an interesting psychological origin. I think the psychological appeal of this is being wanted so badly that someone will do anything to have you. Again, this is not PC to talk about, and I am NOT condoning sexual violence! My point here is to understand that most women do want to be DESIRED. Men have to be careful with this, but I also wanted to normalize the fantasy. Most people are ashamed to admit these things, and only do it on anonymous surveys and in the privacy of therapists offices (if that). I have many clients who have a lot of shame around their sexual fantasies, and much of my work with them is normalizing fantasies.

My point is that most women do want men who take control, and there is a sexy and respectful way to do it. There is a scene in the Netflix show, *Nobody Wants This*, where the male lead, Noah, kisses the female lead, Joanne, for the first time. He tells (not asks) her to put down her ice cream and her bag, in a sexy and confident way, and then kisses her. Watch this scene. She makes a joke later about the kiss being so good she thinks she might be pregnant.

This also does not mean that these women are not feminists and do not believe in female empowerment—quite the opposite. Women can own their sexuality and be confident in their desires as well. People who think these can't coexist are rigid and closed-minded. Women can be feminists and also want to be more on the submissive side in the bedroom. Miranda dates a man who is sort of an asshole in real life, but she talks about how when he tells her what to do in the bedroom, it "REALLY drives [her] crazy."

Note that dominance does NOT mean being an asshole. It means taking control in a sexy, confident, and respectful way. Believe it or not, your wife probably wanted you to be more dominant. This is going to sound silly, but there were probably some clues regarding this: if she, or any other woman, asked you for help with things like reaching something up high, asking for your sweatshirt if she was cold, wanting you to drive, decide on dinner, etc., this likely means she wanted a take-charge partner who is attentive to her needs. Of course, this relates to things like paying on the first date, love languages, etc., that are covered in other chapters. But here I am talking specifically about how to be dominant in bed.

Whether your partner likes a more dominant man would be a very excellent thing to discuss to see if it is something she is into. Yay for communication. But it still can be awkward to do it, especially if you are new to it. But how important is it to go out of your comfort zone? So important! The worst that can happen is a little awkwardness. Best that can happen is a hot sex life. No brainer. Here are a few do's and don'ts when it comes to being more dominant and verbal (which in some ways goes hand-in-hand and a lot of women like as well) in bed.

DO:

- Verbalize what you are going to do to her and what you want her to do ("I'm going to kiss you now." "I'm going to take off your shirt." "Lay down." "Put your hands over your head"). And so on. Do this in a low, calm, confident tone.

- Physically move her around in positions you want her to be in. Respectfully and carefully, but certainly confidently.

- Praise and compliment her. Be very verbal during sex. Most women find this a turn on. Tell her you love her body, she is beautiful, amazing, etc. Say things like "look at you," and "oh my god" when you look at her.

- Ask her if she likes to be called other things in bed. Some women get super turned on by being called degrading names. Definitely get consent on this!!

DO NOT:

- Yell (or talk too loudly).

- Be tentative.

- Repeating this here: Make jokes or be silly during sex. If something funny or awkward happens, definitely laugh, that is not what I mean here. Sex is for sure playful and things happen! I just mean jokes that are not sexy.

- Ask too many questions during sex. Note that this is different than asking what your partner likes in bed and how to get her off. You can ask for feedback in a confident way, which is a turn-on (for example, "you like that?").

Sex can be an amazing area for play and exploration and novelty, and there is a huge range of things to do/explore. A good rule of thumb for sex (and life, frankly, is "don't knock it til you try it!"). Dominance can be extended to BDSM (bondage, dominant/submissive, sadism/masochism) and kink as well, but is not necessarily kinky in itself. If you want more "how-tos" regarding dominance, BDSM, and kink in general, look in the back of the book for more recommendations. I have many couples in my practice who have gotten much closer after a bit of exploration in the bedroom. I also have clients who have found much more sexually compatible partners after their marriages!

FLIPPING THE SCRIPT

What if you are reading this and thinking *"but I actually want to be submissive in bed, not dominant!"* To that I say, cool! Listen, whatever you are into is great. Just make sure no one "yucks your yum." A compatible partner will be open and interested in whatever you want. Don't feel shame just because I just spent a few pages writing about how most women like men who are dominant. There are plenty of women who are more dominant as well. And there are definitely women who "switch."

Even if this does not come naturally to her, if she is someone who is open-minded and likes you and you express love in her love language, she will likely do most things you ask for/express interest in. Do not fall into a trap of kink-shaming yourself, not asking for what you need, and then not being satisfied. Bad trap. Remember, authenticity and openness. If someone judges you, they are not for you!

FOLLOWING UP AFTER SEX

Since this is supposed to be about sex and dating, I will come back to this. Let's say you've been out a couple times, had sex, and either you are feeling it or you are not. Please follow-up (in a timely manner) either way. Communicate if you would like to see her again, and communicate if you don't think it is a good fit or you don't see things moving forward. I promise you that she can handle it. When women regret having sex "too soon," the issue is honestly more so based on the follow-up (or lack thereof) on the part of the man, not on the regret over the sex itself.

If a woman wanted to sleep with you, then she wanted to sleep with you! But please be respectful of this and follow-up either way. If you don't want to see her again, don't worry, I have a whole chapter on how to end things coming up! I saw a post by a woman in the social media group complaining about a man who ghosted after sex on the first date, and a comment justifying this: "This is science, but after intimacy, men produce more testosterone which causes a lot of them to go quiet or pull away for a day or so after it. Give it time. It's SCIENCE, ladies, don't worry." This is obviously fake news! If you've slept together, shoot a text. It's not that hard. No excuses.

I hope this chapter gave you a bit more insight as well as some practical tips around sex. It is truly such an important way to connect in a relationship, and I encourage you to think deeply about all this.

TL;DR

- When dating, there is no "right" time to have sex: Do it when both people want to, but talk about it!
- Condoms are the default until discussed otherwise.
- Be sensitive to women's prior experiences.
- Most women want dominant men in bed.
- There are many "do's" and "don'ts" regarding being dominant in bed.
- Don't yuck anyone's yum, including your own!
- Communicate about sex!
- Follow up after sex.

HOMEWORK

- ☐ Pick one element of this chapter and introspect about this. Think about what you would like to do differently in the future, and start now!
- ☐ Check out some of the recommendations in the back for this chapter.

CHAPTER 12

PORNOGRAPHY

The Truth About the Impact on Relationships

"How's Ethan?" —CARRIE TO MIRANDA
[ASKING ABOUT A GUY SHE IS SEEING]

"Aside from his porn addiction?" —MIRANDA

"Still?" —CARRIE

*"It was kind of sexy at first, but it's getting
borderline humiliating. Move your head here.
Move your head there [so he can see the video
while they are fucking]. Isn't the real thing
more exciting than a tape?"* —MIRANDA

"Maybe it's a force of habit." —CARRIE

*"Sure, but I get the feeling he's more interested
in the video than me. Like he's cheating on me
with them while we're having sex. I don't know.
Am I expecting too much?"* —MIRANDA

"No, you deserve his undivided attention." —CARRIE

This is another example of how this iconic show was so ahead of its time. This episode is actually about cheating and what defines it. They wonder if porn usage "counts" as cheating. In this storyline, Miranda is dating Ethan, a documentary film maker, and porn addict. The first time they sleep together, he turns on the porn as a "sexy" addition. Miranda kinda gets into it. Then, Miranda and Carrie have the above conversation on the street. Ultimately, Miranda has had enough of it and makes him choose, the women in the video or her. Ethan tells her, *"it's not that simple... I've only known you for a few weeks. But I've been involved with some of those women for years."* Miranda promptly exits. This is a shining example of how porn can impact intimacy, and how addictive it really can be. Even though Ethan was using it under the guise of a fun thing to share, it was clear he couldn't get turned on without it. Big problem. We don't learn what happened to him in the end, but unless he got it under control, I'm sure this kept happening! It sabotaged his intimacy and sex life.

PORN/MASTURBATION

I decided to give this topic its own chapter because it is so important! I tend to think about porn as sort of a silent relationship killer. Like alcohol, it is easy to underestimate the impact of it on your relationship. If I'm wrong about this next assumption, sincerest apologies, and you are in the minority. But I am assuming you watched a decent amount of porn in your marriage.

I first want to clarify that my issue with porn is not a moral/ethical one (though it is certainly not without its issues and please do your best to be informed about the ethics around your consumption), but more so as it relates to your relationship, sexuality, and sex drive. This might not surprise you, but Pornhub is in the top five most visited websites, right up there with Google and YouTube. According to a recent metanalysis on porn usage, over 2.5 million people visit pornography sites every 60 seconds (Irizarry et al, 2023).

I personally am not surprised by this, given what I see in my practice. Most men don't volunteer this information in session (unless they are specifically seeking therapy for it, which is actually not infrequent); I have to ask about it in session. Once I do though, there is so much to discuss on it!

I would say—based on my own observations—that most men I see in my practice watch and get off to porn a few times per week. I am mostly talking about men in long-term relationships, and most of these long-term relationships are sexless (defined as having sex once/month on average). Remember, these are just the people I see in my practice, meaning people that are coming for help, so that is not to say that most marriages are sexless.

So, which comes first here, my friends? The chicken or the porn? Hard to say. It's a slippery slope, like many addictive behaviors. Of course, I'm sure you would say that you wouldn't "have to" watch porn if you were having sex! But what IF, heaven forbid, there was no porn? What if (gasp!) you were banned from masturbating altogether by the Lord herself?? Let's just pretend for a moment that the ONLY source of sexual satisfaction you had was your partner. What kind of partner would you be/have been? What would you be doing/have done differently? Really really think about this.

I have so many clients who talk about the beginning of their relationships when they were having so much sex with their partners, and I often point out that a.) they were much younger and had different physiology, b.) responsive desire (refer back to this), but also c.) you were probably doing a whole lot for them that you aren't doing anymore! Everything goes both ways, so deeply introspect about this.

It is way too easy to rely solely on porn for your sexual outlet. Porn teaches you a few things that I believe to be very detrimental to relationships. I believe this is true for all genders, but I will focus here on what it teaches straight men.

First, it teaches men that women are always down for sex, essentially no matter what. It does nothing to educate about responsive desire. There is little to no foreplay in most porn. It also gives an unfair basis for comparison in terms of what most women like in bed. Porn stars fuck like... well, porn stars. I said earlier that most women do not orgasm from being thrown around in a million different positions (that isn't to say that some women don't like that, but porn for sure gives a false impression about the female orgasm).

Porn also portrays women as being able to orgasm multiple times with relative ease. For most women, this is not the case! It takes time and effort and foreplay and serious arousal. I talked about orgasms previously so I won't rehash here, but suffice it to say that porn does not teach men the truth about female orgasms. It sets up men for unrealistic expectations. It also suggests women are down for anything and everything.

Remember, that these actors are just that. They literally get paid to be good at this stuff. I'm sure you could deepthroat for 30 minutes straight if you got paid to do it and practiced all the time.

Now here's the thing, I know you don't really expect your partner to fuck (or look, for that matter), like a porn star. I can totally appreciate that. And I definitely tell my female clients that. Women are often self-conscious because they are worried that men expect them to look like a porn star, which could be yet another reason for your lackluster sex life (body image issues on the part of the woman). In my experience, men don't actually expect that. I'm sure you just wanted affection, attention, sex, and a blowjob sometimes. But these messages DO make their way into your subconscious. If your comparison is women who fuck for the world to see, then of course your wife is going to seem "frigid" by comparison. Just food for thought regarding the effect of porn on your expectations around sex.

I see many clients who have changed their life and relationships when they stopped watching porn, or significantly cut down. They are being more intimate with their partners, having more sex, touching more, and being more emotionally vulnerable. When my clients stop watching porn, many of them also realize they have an artificially inflated sex drive when they are consuming porn. This means that their sex drive was not actually as high as they thought it was when they were constantly masturbating. It would be akin to craving sugar when you are constantly eating donuts—more begets more.

As they stop watching porn/masturbating, many of them realize they actually prefer going to bed early with their wives and chatting with them, and yes, having sex sometimes too, but they found they don't need it as often as they thought. Overall, they reported the connection to be much more fulfilling. Makes total sense!

In case you have questions about my stance on pornography (in sexless relationships), I'll keep going. I like to use the analogy of Chick-fil-A. Bear with me, I'm not homophobic, I just love their nuggets. It's way too easy not to be hungry for a nice meal when you get home if you stopped for nuggets along the way. Sometimes it feels like a mountain to climb to take the time to cook a nice meal with your wife, especially if it's been a while. But what is more satisfying in the long run? A nice meal where you cook together, enjoy it together, talk about it later, etc., or a quick stop by and eat in the car on the way home? Fine, sometimes it IS those delish nuggets. But I'm sure you would rather have had an incredible sex life with your wife. It seems impossible when you are so disconnected, and porn is right there at your fingertips and can give you exactly what you want in the moment.

When I ask men this in sessions (to be clear, the option is porn/masturbating vs. great connected sex with your wife), no one has EVER said that is not the case. One caveat to this is unless you have never been attracted to your partner, which is obviously a huge problem. The next time around, prioritize attraction. BUT, even with long-term monogamy, aging, etc., the men who are attracted to their wives will choose the "elaborate meal" 100% of the time. Of course, if things are so bad, you are not going to want to have sex with your wife, so that's the other caveat. Like a client told me once, "I can't get it up for angry." The emotional connection matters with men too, despite what society would have us think.

The last issue with porn, and possibly masturbation in general, is that masturbation can actually build a tolerance in the sense of the physical sensation. If you know exactly how to touch/grip yourself to make yourself orgasm, your penis might actually be desensitized to orgasming from oral sex or penetration, which does not have as tight of a grip as your hand. This is the case sometimes with women and vibrators. You can actually retrain yourself to orgasm from different stimulation, but just something to consider.

I equate porn for men to romance novels/movies/TV/social media, etc. for women. It sets up unrealistic expectations for men around romance, the same way I think it does for women around sex. HOWEVER, as I discuss in the next chapter, a level of sex and romance is incredibly important and totally doable in relationships. So, we actually CAN learn something from porn and romance novels! Blowjobs and love letters, my friends. Both possible and great.

In sum, think about your porn habits in the past and currently. If you are single, it's probably not hurting anyone, though it might be artificially inflating your libido, and you might be conditioning yourself to require a certain type of physical touch, which can affect your sex life with a partner. It also might impact motivation to go out and date, in sort of the same way it is easier to stop for fast food than to make a nice meal. But you are missing out on the opportunity for real-life connections. The takeaway: Make it a goal to be as open about sex and what you like moving forward, with the goal of a loving and fulfilling sex life! How great would it be if most of your physical/sexual needs would be met by your partner and not the internet? It can happen! This is discussed more in the next chapter on love languages.

TL;DR

- Porn can be detrimental to intimacy for many reasons. That's the TL;DR!

HOMEWORK

☐ Really think about your porn/masturbation habits. If you are in a relationship, try to cut back on it.

CHAPTER 13

LOVE LANGUAGES

The Key to Stronger Connections

"I'm a trisexual. I'll try anything once." —SAMANTHA

I chose this quote because in addition to it being the epitome of Samantha Jones, it is super important when thinking about love languages! The motto of "trying anything once" extends well beyond sex and is so important for successful relationships. In this chapter, I will talk generally about the importance of love languages and go through each one, and end with some final thoughts on this (very important!) concept.

Unless you have truly been living under a rock, you know about the "Five Love Languages." The love languages were actually developed thirty years ago by a Baptist Pastor, Dr. Gary Chapman, who noticed common themes among the couples that he counseled. He noticed that people have different ways of giving and receiving love, and he categorized them into five main categories. I'm going to describe the five main categories here and provide my personal opinion on them from what I see every day in my practice. A quick preamble: The important thing to understand about love languages is that you need to think about them in terms of how one RECEIVES love, not how one GIVES love. Remember the "blowjobs and love letters" comparison from chapter one. More on this after an overview.

WORDS OF AFFIRMATION

This means that you feel most loved and appreciated by receiving not only compliments, but deep explanations of where those affirmative words are coming from. If words of affirmation is your love language, in addition to face-to-face affirmations, you likely also love reading love notes and cards written for you that talk about why you are so great, what someone loves about you, visions for the future with you, and memories of the past with you. You feel very loved when you read/hear statements like:

"When I met you I felt_____."

"You are an amazing parent because _____."

"I am so lucky to have you."

"You are the only one that can do _____ for me."

"I don't know what I would do without you."

"You are so [smart, beautiful, sexy, kind, generous, etc.]."

"You are a great friend."

"I can't wait for _____ in the future."

"Our/your kids are the luckiest kids in the world to have you as their parent."

"You are brilliant."

"You've changed me for the better."

"I'm so glad I met you."

"You are enough; you are more than enough."

"I love you just the way you are."

"You make me a better person."

"I can't imagine my life without you."

"I love when you do _____ for me."

"I feel like my best self around you."

"You are killing it at [XYZ] task."

...to name a few. Obviously, not all of the ones listed will be applicable, but those are just examples of the things people want to hear if they have this love language.

A quick word on words. These must be genuine, and beware of being too heavy-handed early on in a relationship. A lot of women like compliments and like to hear these bigger sentiments, but can certainly tell if they are not authentic, and a lot of them can't be said if you don't really know the person. So, just think on this. If it is a long-term partner and you never say anything like the examples above, introspect about it. If your wife told you did not appreciate her, it is likely she meant that you were not effusive with the expressions of appreciation, gratitude, and compliments.

Barring it being too soon in a relationship, when your partner has a words of affirmation love language, there is not really a "too much." You might have thought, *Well, my wife knows she is beautiful, why do I have to say it all the time?* This would be like saying, *I gave you a kiss last week, why do you need another one??* if your love language is physical touch (more below). There's no such thing as a "words of affirmation" ceiling. The exception to this is what I mentioned before about it being inauthentic, too soon, or from a pre-occupied attachment place (*she won't love me unless I tell her this all the time*, for example). Outside of that, lay it on!

These types of expressions should happen at least daily, if not more frequently. I have a client who retells his wife the story of them meeting every year for their anniversary, spending 20-30 minutes on every detail, and she loves it. It's a great gift!

GIFTS

Fairly self-explanatory, though I will still explain, because this love language often gets a bad rap. When people have a love language of receiving gifts, it is truly about the thought behind the gifts. It is not about the expense. That is not to say that someone can't like both, but many people feel very connected, seen, and special when gifts are bought for them. Of course, this can include more extravagant stuff for holidays/birthdays/anniversaries, but it also means little thoughtful things on a regular basis. Did you get that? A REGULAR basis.

For example, their favorite ice cream from the grocery store, or a framed photo of the kids on a random Tuesday because you all did something fun over the weekend, or a snow-globe from the airport when you are traveling. This signals that you are thinking about the person, and that you KNOW them and their tastes.

Many women I see in my practice feel very loved when their husbands get them gifts that reflect them, and conversely very unseen if they don't. A friend of mine's husband knows how much she loves shows on Bravo (and he does too), and got her a cameo of one of her favorite "Bravolebrities" for their anniversary.

Gifts that are appreciated are usually thoughtful and tend to be on the romantic side, like flowers or something sentimental. Gifts that are not super appreciated are things like household items, unless it is a very specific thing that your partner has been asking for. Also, generic gifts that are just given to check boxes are not appreciated. The weeks after Mother's Day and Father's Day are very busy for me in my practice, because there are so many bad gifts given (i.e. a fancy comb).

If you are dating/partnered with someone whose love language is gifts, make it a point to get something small every few weeks (many clients even put this on their calendar! It IS that important), and listen when your partner is telling you they want something. For example, if your partner complains that all her socks have holes in them, or they have been meaning to try a new wine, buy them new socks and that wine as a surprise on a random day! This will make them feel incredibly special and hardly takes any time/resources. Well worth the "investment"! It also signals that you are listening, paying attention, and remembering.

QUALITY TIME

This means that the way you feel loved is by quality time with your partner! This can look many different ways, from a long vacation together to date night to working out together to talking for twenty minutes in the evenings to dropping off the kids together to cleaning the house together (yes, this can totally be quality time!!). Almost any activity that you do together can be quality time, if you are also focused on the relationship while you are doing the task (even a mundane errand can be fulfilling for someone whose love language is quality time).

Another important note on this love language: the time together is not "quality" if one person is looking at their phone the entire time. Five minutes of uninterrupted time without phones is more fulfilling than two hours of time together where one or both people are staring at their screens (for example, over dinner or watching a show).

This is a good time to talk about how I see a lot of people in my practice prioritize "dividing and conquering" over quality time. For example, one person will run errands while one person will take the kids to the park. This might be more "efficient," but for someone with this love language, it is very disconnecting to do this all the time.

Errands/chores can be romantic and connecting! It makes you feel like a team. It is often important to prioritize quality time over efficiency and feel like a team doing things together, especially if you are with someone with this love language.

PHYSICAL TOUCH

This one also gets a bad rap, especially for men. It's reduced to "men just want to fuck." This can be incredibly problematic for men whose love language is physical touch, which, from my experience, is many. Maybe 97%. And the remaining 3% perhaps don't know that it is their love language. Kidding. Mostly.

Many people feel loved with touch! This certainly includes sex but is definitely not limited to it. Hand holding, kissing, cuddling, massage, head/back scratches, hugs, arms around each other, etc., are all under the umbrella of physical touch (non-sexual physical touch, or NSPT).

People with this love language need physical intimacy—in all its forms—to feel close. Typically, men who have physical touch love languages also have high sex drives, which is also imperative for closeness and connection. The men I see in my practice who are not getting physical touch from their wives feel incredibly misunderstood and lonely. They often feel gross or needy asking for this (and have typically been rejected many times), so they don't, and as a result can feel sad, lonely, neglected, and unloved.

As a culture, we discount this love language and it really is a shame. We emphasize acts of service, as if taking out the trash is more important than a hug. Would you turn down your child's need for physical affection? Likely no. It is also the only love language that cannot be outsourced within a monogamous relationship. Which means if you are not getting touched in your relationship, you just aren't getting love in the way you need it.

There might be a lot of people who tell you that you are a great dad, colleague, friend, etc., and that could fulfill the words of affirmation language, for example. You can also have someone else make (or deliver) dinner. But this one cannot be outsourced. So, if this was a problem in your marriage, find someone whose love language is also physical touch, or at the very least has an excellent understanding of these concepts.

I'm going to take a minute here to talk about why I see a big decline in physical touch in long-term relationships. In addition to sex and kissing, non-sexual physical touch also declines over time. I'm guessing this happened in your marriage. There can be many reasons for this, but I'll give you one common one. Often, your wife/long term partner will associate physical touch from you with a desire for sex, and she does not want to have sex.

Refer back to my responsive desire section for more on this; however, it is likely that if your marriage ended it was more than sex drive waning in long-term monogamy. If there was pressure to have sex (likely unintended), then your ex-wife probably associated any physical touch with an expectation or a desire for sex (which by the way, is a fine desire, as I've said multiple times!). If she ever commented on being "touched out," this is a good indicator of this.

Most people are not "touched out" on relaxing, warm, nice touches that feel good and don't come with strings (real or imagined). If she ever went to get a professional massage, this is proof of this. She was "touched out" from kids hanging on her and from expectations of sex from you. If every time she was touched, she associated it with expectations, she probably bristled away, which of course does not feel good for you. You likely felt rejected, offended, disconnected. The more this happens over time, the less touch there is overall, which isn't actually what either partner wants.

An analogy might help with this. It would be like if your ex had a love language of acts of service, and loved when you made dinner for her, and every time you were in the kitchen at all she was asking you if you were going to make her dinner. If you walked into the kitchen for a snack she would say "oh yay! What are you making me??" This would make you feel a lot of pressure, and you would learn to avoid the kitchen. Same reason she avoided physical touch.

Another reason could be because she did not like the way you touched her. She might not have liked if you grabbed her, or tickled her, or if you had bad hygiene she also probably bristled. All things to think about.

Important takeaways here. If touch is important to you, make sure to do LOTS of non-sexual physical touch in your next relationships, with someone who also values it. Hold hands, give massages, cuddle... all without expectations of sex. Just make it part of a routine of intimacy. Do it so she feels good and relaxed as well, and not as a means to an end. A healthy, intimate relationship has lots of non-sexual physical touch in addition to lots of sexual activity.

Because love languages are all the rage now, it can be very tempting to advertise this in a dating app. Do not say that your love language is physical touch. Or "cuddles." People will assume that you "just" want to fuck. *But* [you might say], *it's an important part of the relationship and someone I am dating needs to know that!* Yes. And they will. In time. In the next chapter, I discuss how to tell if a woman is sexually compatible, but for many women it is a turn-off to see it on a profile.

ACTS OF SERVICE

When one has an acts of service love language, they love when things are taken off their plate. This can mean things like planning (and executing) dinners for the week, cleaning the kitchen, packing lunches, organizing the finances, planning vacation ideas, putting gas in the car, driving to/from the airport, building furniture, running errands, booking babysitters, etc.

This is a widely accepted one in our culture, and a lot of women have this love language (especially women with young kids! In fact, I've never encountered a mom with young kids whose love language was not acts of service, though that might not be the only one).

A pretty important part of this love language is anticipating the thing that needs to be done, and taking initiative to do it yourself. Women complain all the time that their husbands are sitting down while they are getting things ready around the house, getting the kids together, etc., and all they want is their husbands to take initiative and get the kids dressed. *"But Elana, every time I get the kids dressed, she tells me I do it wrong!"* Yes. I hear you. That is also problematic, and criticism is not great. BUT. If it is important to her that the kids wear something specific, just do that thing. She will be very happy and feel loved and... wait for it... be much more generous with YOUR love language. Do you honestly care about their outfits?

This is not about being a "yes man." This is about being agreeable and laid-back and knowing what is important to your partner. An example of an acts of service gift for a holiday or birthday would be setting aside time to do a house-project your partner has been asking you to do, and telling her your plan to do it so she is aware. Remember, go above and beyond on holidays (i.e. making a list of possible kid gifts, planning travel, etc.), birthdays, etc., but there are opportunities for acts of service all the time!

Think back on your marriage. What are some things your wife asked you to do that you might have not completed (for whatever reason)? This is hard to think about but important! YOU might not care if the dishes are clean or the counter is wiped down a certain way, but if she does, that's what matters. Every time you DON'T do that thing, she feels like you don't care how she feels. She feels unloved and disrespected; like her wants/needs don't matter. Again, I refer you to Matthew Fray's essay.

This is a really important takeaway. This is obviously a theme throughout this book: the thing that is important to her might not be important to you, and vice versa.

LOVE-BOMBING

A quick word on love-bombing. Though I just spend the majority of this chapter discussing the importance of knowing and speaking each other's love languages, these things take time. "Love bombing" refers to very grand and excessive romantic gestures in the beginning of the relationship before you really get to know each other. When done intentionally, this is a manipulation tactic to keep control in the relationship. However, I often see this done unintentionally and as a result of insecurity and anxious attachment.

More on developing a relationship that lasts in the next chapter, but for now it is important to point out that showing love needs to develop in a consistent and authentic way, from a place of secure attachment. If you find yourself extremely compelled to do these "grand gestures" early on, this is a flag that you might be moving too quickly and it is less about the person and more about you not wanting to be alone (i.e. anxious attachment).

A GENERAL WORD ON LOVE LANGUAGES

Some people deny the importance of these and say they are not real. They are as real as liking dogs or not liking dogs, or beach vs. mountain people, for example. They are about preferences, and the people who say they are not "real," often have trouble understanding other people's perspectives. Even one of the husbands (the best one IMO) on *The Valley* on Bravo stated the importance of them! Thanks for spreading the gospel, Danny.

It is truly imperative that you know your own love language as well as your partner's love language. What I mean by that is knowing how one RECEIVES love, not how one SHOWS love. Both are important in understanding yourself and each other, but in order to feel fully loved and fulfilled, you have to know what makes you feel that way!

I do think there are probably more than five love languages; in fact there might even be hundreds. But it doesn't really matter. How we default to giving love is often a reflection of how we receive it. For example, if someone shows love by writing handwritten cards telling someone why they love them, that is likely reflective of a words of affirmation love language for them, meaning THEY would like to receive handwritten cards.

I have had so many couple's sessions where the wife is disappointed the husband doesn't appreciate their handwritten cards for birthdays, anniversaries, etc., and the husband is disappointed that there was no sex for these occasions. I typically explain to them that it's because it (the card) is not their husband's love language. They might appreciate it, but they don't feel unloved without it; whereas, if the wife doesn't get a handwritten card, they would feel unloved. Same goes for the aforementioned acts of service.

I can't tell you how many times I've heard from women some variation of "I spent all day cleaning and he doesn't even appreciate it!" Well, it might not be important to your partner, so of course, he doesn't appreciate as much as she would if he spent all day cleaning the house because he knew it's important to her.

One more example because this is all so important. Let's say your partner's love language is fun dates (acts of service and quality time), and you ask them when they are free, get tickets to a show you know she would like, and make a dinner reservation, she will likely be very happy! She would also be much more willing to have sex later (or the next day) even if she is tired and not really feeling it. If, however, she is the one making the plans, getting the tickets, etc., it will be much harder for her to get in the mood because she doesn't feel like you went out of your way to show her love. It's one thing to go along with her plans, but it truly shows love if there is initiative.

This is why so many men complain they don't even have sex on date nights! When I ask them who planned the date, they will say their wives. How could they possibly expect their wife to try to get in the mood when they are the ones looking at the calendar, booking the babysitter, finding a reservation, etc.

Incidentally, this is often why men appreciate it so much when women initiate sex, because they know they are going out of their way to do something important to them that they maybe would not initiate on their own.

Furthermore, and this point deserves its own section, you can't expect them to be open-minded and adventurous in bed if you are not open-minded and excited about what they want to do outside of the bedroom. This is where Samantha's "trisexual" quote is relevant. For example, I have clients complain that their wives won't mix it up or do a certain act (this is typically either oral or anal sex) in the bedroom, and I ask them if there are things their wife wants them to do that they shut down, and invariably they will say something like, "well, I refuse to go to the ballet with her." See! How can you expect open-mindedness re: sex when you shoot down what is important to her! This goes for shows, books, "cheesy" activities, etc.

I have had many clients see noticeable increases in sex and physical intimacy in general after they started regularly planning fun, new activities for their partners. An important note here. This is NOT about "tit for tat," as many clients are worried about. It is about love languages and truly feeling generous with showing love when one is feeling loved themselves. One cannot express their love in the other person's love language if they are not receiving love in theirs.

Take a moment to reflect on this in the context of your marriage. What was your wife's love language? Did you miss the mark on this? Did you take her requests to be controlling? Unimportant? Hopefully, after reading this, you have a better understanding of the importance of love languages and how to make a partner feel truly loved.

What is YOUR love language? Did you feel like you were not able to express it? Were you dismissed or shut down? This is a perfect time to introspect on all this and learn for the next time! Relationships are happiest when people have similar love languages, because it comes more naturally for both people and they don't have to work as hard/think as much to express love in a way that is more foreign to them. There are ways to discern this up front (more on this later).

Relationships can still be successful with differing love languages; people just have to talk about it! They have to understand their own and each other's and be open-minded and non-judgmental of the thing that is important to the other person.

TOOT YOUR OWN HORN

I briefly touched on this idea earlier in the "looking back" chapter, but moving forward in your relationships, it is really important to not only speak in the other person's love language, but to let them know when you do so! Otherwise, you are not directly telling them you are thinking about them, which is the whole point of love languages.

So, for example, if you buy tickets to a show that you yourself would never want to see, TELL HER something like, "hey I got us tickets to see [whatever it is] because I know how much you'd love it and I want you to know I was thinking about you!" or "hey, I skipped watching the game with my friends today to hang out with you because I love you so much!"

Share these things. You are losing important opportunities for closeness and connection if you don't share what you are doing for your partner. This isn't bragging; this is communicating. Toot away!

TL;DR

- Love language refers to how one receives love, not how one gives it.
- Words of affirmation include compliments and deep authentic expressions of love and gratitude, plus reminiscing about the past and talking about the future.
- Gifts refers to thoughtful gifts on a regular basis, and going above and beyond for special occasions.
- Quality time can (and should!) include things like errands AND date nights/vacations. Put the phone down during quality time.
- Physical Touch is often discounted but is arguably the most important within monogamy. This is not limited to sex, but also includes hand holding, hugs, snuggling, kissing, massages, and back scratches.

- Acts of service refers to having things taken off your plate.

- Do not confuse showing someone love with "love bombing" in the initial stages of a relationship.

- It's all about anticipating and initiating love in your partner's love language.

- Toot your own horn!

HOMEWORK

☐ Think about your love language(s) and that of your previous partner's. If you don't already know yours, take an online quiz!

☐ Make a list of your ex's love language and some examples of how you did not show her love this way. Part of the purpose of this book is to have you introspect on the tough stuff so you don't make the same mistakes! Takes two to tango, my friends.

CHAPTER 14

GETTING SERIOUS

Building a Relationship That Lasts

"They say that opposites attract, but they never say for how long. Should the relationship-savvy person stoke the fires of passion with the kindling of work and friends or should we simply be satisfied with a romance that sizzles? I couldn't help but wonder— without sharing your worlds, could even the hottest relationship stop cold?" —CARRIE BRADSHAW

Yes. The answer to this question is yes. In this episode, Carrie is musing about her relationship with Aleksandr Petrovsky, where she at one point tells Miranda that they "don't really have anything in common but each other." Chemistry, and NRE (discussed in this chapter), is certainly important, but not enough to sustain a long-term relationship. Compatibility is everything. In this chapter, I will discuss the beginnings of relationships as well as what to look for in terms of compatibility.

Eventually (typically) either the relationship becomes more serious, or you break up (which I cover in the next chapter). Here, I want to provide some things to think about to help determine if someone is a good fit for you for the long term. Now, this sort of assumes you are ready for that, which, you might not be at this point. But nonetheless, it's important to think about for when you are! I will cover New Relationship Energy (NRE), what to look for in terms of compatibility, defining the relationship (DTR), exclusivity, and non-monogamy. Of note! Many of these topics do not have a "one size fits all" approach, so I discuss general principles to keep in mind throughout the progression of a relationship.

NEW RELATIONSHIP ENERGY (NRE)

NRE is essentially the drug of a new relationship. Your brain is being flooded with dopamine, serotonin, and oxytocin. Remember the old, "this is your brain on drugs" commercials? That's what I think about. You are on a drug when you are falling in love. It is both a beautiful thing and a dangerous thing.

Typically, with NRE, you are wanting to spend a lot of time with this new person, you are excited all the time, thinking about them all the time, perhaps you are sleeping less and/or missing work or other responsibilities to see them. If you are having sex, you are probably doing it a lot. There is nothing wrong with NRE and it can be really incredible! However. Please recognize it for what it is. This is the "honeymoon phase," and it typically lasts about 18 months (give or take).

There are a few important things to keep in mind while you are in the land of NRE: one, getting along while in NRE does not mean long-term compatibility. It is very easy to overlook red flags during this stage of a relationship. Don't mistake great sex and physical attraction for compatibility. Chemistry is "necessary but not sufficient" for a successful long-term relationship.

WHAT TO AVOID DURING NRE

Avoid making any major life decisions during this "honeymoon phase." For example, don't move across the country, quit your job, decide to have a kid, etc. Not getting caught up in NRE is especially important if you have kids and are deciding when to integrate your lives. Especially when you are separated, it is extremely important to be cautious when getting into another relationship.

I've said this before, and although it varies, I would say a good rule-of-thumb would be to avoid anything serious until at least a year AFTER your divorce is final. Because of all the reasons discussed in this book, it is virtually impossible to be in a place where you can be a stable, secure, reliable, loving partner during such a tumultuous time. You need to get through your divorce and adjust to your new life, and that takes a lot of focus on yourself, your kids (if applicable), and energy. The work you put in during this time will greatly benefit you in the next relationship, when the time is right!

I discuss important areas of compatibility (the tl;dr on that is, they are mostly all important) to make sure they are present before you make major decisions about a new relationship (in addition, of course, to all the great work you are doing on yourself and your confidence). As you are getting to know each other, you can start incorporating each other into your life in ways that feel right. For example, meeting friends, other family, traveling, etc. These are all good ways to also assess compatibility.

Here are some additional questions to think about when you are considering a future with someone:

- Do you fit well into each other's lives?

- Do you feel similarly regarding when to start blending your lives?

- Is one person more invested than the other?

- Is planning things easy or difficult?

- Is decision-making often a problem, or is it relatively seamless?

Another plug for *Love is Blind* here (sorry not sorry) for great examples of couples figuring out how to merge their lives after they fall in love. Contestants date each other and fall in love behind a wall, which in theory is supposed to remove the superficial aspect of dating and emphasis on appearance that many people prioritize. The question is, can people fall in love without ever seeing each other? Sure they can. However, the problem with this premise, of course, is that a.) attraction actually does matter and b.) the contestants fall in love before they get a chance to see if they are 1.) attracted and 2.) real-world compatible. For example, after they meet, they might hate each other's style, or how they decorate their apartment, or their friends. All of these scenarios have happened and the couples in those situations don't last. These things really matter for the long haul.

WHAT TO LOOK FOR IN TERMS OF COMPATIBILITY AS THE RELATIONSHIP PROGRESSES

Sexual Compatibility

While you are on the drug of NRE, I implore you to still consider important elements of compatibility that will remain after the "zsa zsa zsu" fades (thank you again, Carrie Bradshaw).

186

Starting with the physical stuff, here are a few ways to tell if a woman is into sex and physical touch in the same way you are from early on (some of these seem obvious but stating them anyway!):

- if she describes herself as a sexual person, which includes bringing sex up on her own, talking about what she is into, past experiences, etc.;

- if she is touchy in general;

- if she seems open-minded in general and is not grossed out easily (food is actually a good example here).

Of course, they could be sexual and not be into you! Don't ask them about this directly (meaning, for example, if you have to ask if they are a sexual person, you probably have your answer). If, early on, you don't have a similar drive (i.e. one person wants to have sex several times per day/week and the other one doesn't or one person wants to go again quickly and the other rarely does), are not into the same general things (i.e. oral, different positions, using toys, etc.), can't talk openly about what you are into, if watching sex scenes on TV or in movies is awkward, and for SURE if she is judgmental about anything you like/have done/want to try, these are all major red flags for sexual incompatibility, and for a lack of open-mindedness in general.

Do not pursue a relationship with someone you are not sexually compatible with. It never ends well; you will end up dissatisfied and your partner will feel guilty and bad about herself.

Be yourself and be authentic—no shame in what you like! This goes for anything, as I mentioned when discussing your dating profile, but it is true especially for sex among men who have a physical touch love language. If you are not open about what you want, how could you ever get it? You'll never know that you can be truly accepted for who you are if you are not being your authentic self!

As discussed, sexual desire among women decreases in monogamy, so it's incredibly important to start off strong in this realm. You must leave a decent margin of error here, so there is room for the inevitable decline within monogamy. I don't mean to be doomsday about it, it's just what happens in monogamy! If more people knew this, it would be much better. It doesn't mean you won't still be attracted to someone years later and still have great sex; it just means it is different than the initial NRE phase.

The takeaway is: IF this is important to you, find someone who you are SUPER attracted to, who you have great chemistry with, who likes sex as much as you do (even if it is not her primary love language, refer to previous chapter), and who has a similar erotic blueprint. This will save you a lot of heartache later. In my experience, if you have to wonder if someone is interested in sex in the first few dates, the answer is probably not, at least not to the level you are, if the interest is high.

On the other hand, though, sex drive decreases with age, overall. If you are 45, you don't have the same drive you did when you were 30. Sexual functioning decreases too, which is normal! You might not be able to get an erection as easily, orgasm as frequently, have longer refractory periods, etc. This is all completely normal. So, if you are reading this and thinking, *but I have a LOWER sex drive than I used to, and it's just not as important to me anymore,* that's cool too! Again, all about compatibility. A satisfying sex life might look a lot different as you age, but physical connection might still be important. This might look like more non-sexual physical touch, and sex a few times a month vs. a few times a week when you were younger.

Other compatibilities:

Things like: extraversion, open-mindedness, agreeableness, religion, culture, socioeconomic status, interest in travel, night owl/early bird, etc. The more similar you are, the easier, honestly. This sounds a bit boring, but it is not. People romanticize the idea of "opposites attract," or people "complimenting each other," but truthfully it's just easier if you are similar.

Of course you won't be the same person (and you don't need to be!), and you don't have to have all the same interests, but the more similarly you approach things, the better. For example, you don't have to explain why you want to leave a party early, you don't have to argue over a movie or a type of vacation, or whatever it is. You understand each other more.

Yes, compromise is important, but the more different you are, the more each of you has to compromise, and ultimately the less happy you will be. If both of you love the beach, great! If one of you loves the beach and one hates the sand, so you end up skiing as a "compromise" but both of you don't LOVE skiing... who really wins here? So, the more you have in common, the better.

Often, when people meet after divorce, they learn a lot from previous experiences and know what to look for regarding compatibility! Think about these dimensions of compatibility while you are in the NRE phase, and think about how they will play out for the long haul. It also helps to agree on major things like where you want to live and if you want more kids.

Talk about these things early on and be upfront, like every-thing else. I have a client who was contemplating marrying his long-term girlfriend, who really wanted to get married. He was not sure if they were compatible, and he cited liking different grocery stores as an example of an incompatibility. According to him, his girlfriend thought that was pretty ridiculous. In the end, they decided not to get married. Now, of course, it was not about the difference in grocery store preference per se, but it WAS indicative of more fundamental incompatibilities.

And of course... communication!

You must be able to talk to someone you are dating, about basi-cally everything. Nothing should be off the table. This includes past experiences, fears, fantasies, etc. Ask yourself: Are they easy to talk to? Non-defensive? Quick to take responsibility and apologize when things come up? Curious about you? Can you openly ask for what you want?

It is also really important to have open conversations about po-tential dealbreakers, with the goal of assessing compatibility. If you aren't sure you are in the area for the long haul, say that. If you definitely want more kids (or definitely don't), say that. Same goes for marriage, finances, sex, religion, etc.

There is no precise "how to" with these conversations, it's just about being direct. It is more about believing in yourself that you can say the hard things and find people that fit well with those things. Hopefully, you've had conversations about big topics before you get too deep in the relationship. That said, there are some relationship topics that are important to talk about, including "defining the relationship" and ending things, that I can provide some guidance on.

DEFINING THE RELATIONSHIP (DTR)

Before I talk about HOW to "DTR", let me talk about WHEN to DTR. First, I will say that this section applies mostly to people who are wanting monogamous relationships. There is a section below on consensual non-monogamy, though the same general principles of openness and directness apply.

In keeping with the general principles I've been talking about, basically this should happen when it feels right. HOWEVER, if after two dates you want to be exclusive and you want to ask her to be exclusive, I would think deeply about the motivation here. Is it insecure attachment, which basically means motivated by anxiety that she will leave or find someone else? You can make it known you are interested without being in a hurry to be exclusive. You can also decide for yourself if you want to stop dating other people (or not start, depending on what your current "dance card" looks like), but not have the same expectations for her.

If you have a secure attachment and are confident with what you bring to the table (as I've said before, this will likely take time and some experience), you will not be in a hurry for her to be exclusive, because you will be confident that you'll be fine if she doesn't want that! A few months is probably a reasonable amount of time to determine your compatibility, though you know early on if you like someone and are attracted to them.

You probably know pretty quickly if you are attracted to someone or not. It's possible you were not even attracted to your ex-wife, but you married her for other reasons (i.e. maybe you knew she would be a good mom, she treated you well, you subconsciously—or consciously—pretended that attraction wasn't important because you didn't want to be "shallow," societal or family pressure, etc. These all require introspection).

She may have subconsciously reminded you of a family member and things felt like "home."

I discussed this in the therapy chapter earlier, but certainly continue to think about why you might have been drawn to your wife. *Getting the Love you Want* by Harville Hendrix is an excellent resource on why we are drawn to people that remind us of our caregivers. Imago theory states that we are subconsciously drawn to people who have qualities in our caregivers that we were never able to change growing up. These qualities often stopped us from getting the love we want, so we are subconsciously drawn to people who exhibit similar qualities, thinking we can change them.

For example, if you had an angry parent growing up, and this anger prevented them from being loving toward you, and you tried (and failed) to make them less angry, you will be subconsciously drawn to someone who exhibits similar traits of anger in the hopes of changing them into someone who is less angry and can give you the love you want. This is a whole other massive topic, but just wanted to put it on your radar to consider.

Anyway. Moving forward, do not waste your time with someone to whom you are not attracted. There is a lid for every pot, and if you don't find this person attractive, someone else will! Your attraction will not likely grow, and you both deserve better than that. Even if it seems like an insignificant detail or seems shallow, it doesn't matter. I had a client who did not like his date's shoes. This is important. This is indicative of not liking someone's style, of not wanting to "show off" that person. This will take a huge toll on their self-esteem if you're not attracted to them.

You aren't a bad person for having preferences. I get a lot of male clients who are not attracted to people they are dating and feel shallow ending the relationship because of it. Trust me, you are not doing anyone any favors by staying with someone you are lukewarm—or worse—about. It's much worse if you ignore this or attempt to convince yourself it doesn't matter.

Most people have a "type," and they are the happiest when they are dating their type. Sure, there are exceptions. If you meet someone and you really connect, "type" might not matter as much. But there is a feeling of fulfillment that accompanies dating your type, and both people tend to be very happy in those relationships.

In fact, both men and women are happiest in relationships when the man is VERY attracted to the woman from the beginning (type or not), and the woman is considered "the hot one." Women like to feel sexy and desired, and they know when their partners aren't experiencing them that way. It leads to a lot of insecurities and lack of confidence. And men generally don't get the love they want when they are not super attracted. So, don't get serious with someone you aren't deeply attracted to.

DTR AND EXCLUSIVITY

If you do decide you want to be serious with someone, how to DTR? Often, this will come up naturally. Especially if both of you have been/are dating other people (for example, if you met on an app, you can assume both of you are dating), things happen to prompt the conversation. For example, someone gets asked on a date or has plans with someone else that were planned earlier on. Talk about this stuff. If she asks you if you are seeing anyone else or if you plan to, be honest. She is asking! Don't lie. Talk about it.

If you have a history of lying in your marriage, this is also a good time to think about that. Lying is an issue to work on in therapy that is likely related to your upbringing, you wanting to be seen a certain way, not wanting to disappoint someone, or your insecurities around who you are (to name a few). Lying by omission is also lying.

If you are dating multiple people and they would be surprised to find this out, this is lying. This often comes up around sex and talking about safe sex, which should be an open discussion.

If you are considering being exclusive with someone and they ask you if you are seeing other people, they probably have the right to know. If it's just a few dates, different story. If it starts to feel icky and if you find yourself being cagey, this is a sign to talk about it, or a sign that you aren't that into her, and you should consider ending the relationship. However, they should have all the information so they can decide if they want to keep seeing you. There are important themes of honesty and respect here. More on honesty and breaking up in the next chapter!

If nothing naturally prompts the conversation of exclusivity, when you feel like you want to be exclusive and you would like her to consider doing the same, you can say something like, "I've really liked hanging out with you and I want to see where this goes if we just focus on each other. What do you think about that?" This is stating firmly and directly what you want, and then asking her what she thinks. You don't need to be wishy-washy and insecure and ask if she is seeing other people, just say firmly that you want to date exclusively. This shows confidence, rather than asking something like "what are we?"

Remember, if she doesn't want to date you exclusively, someone else will! If she asks you "what you are," answer honestly about where your head is at. If you don't know, that's ok! Just be honest about that and let her decide how she wants to proceed.

SITUATIONSHIPS, FRIENDS WITH BENEFITS (FWBS), AND FUCK BUDDIES

A "situationship" is essentially an undefined relationship that usually consists of at least sex and maybe hanging out, dates, meeting friends, etc., but things are undefined in terms of exclusivity or "labels" of boyfriend/girlfriend. They are undefined either because it is explicitly agreed upon that it is not a serious relationship, or one person wants something more serious and the other doesn't. This can be pretty blurry/complicated, or it can be low-pressure. Just make sure you are open about where you are at, and let people decide for themselves if they want to be in that dynamic.

These typically are not super sustainable because one person is not getting what they need/want from the relationship. People who stay in situationships where they are unhappy often have low self-esteem because they do not think they can find someone who will give them what they want! This is not true! If this sounds like you, definitely consider therapy! It will make you feel worse to stay in something where you are not getting your needs met.

Everyone deserves love and fulfillment, and if you are accepting the bare minimum, please introspect about this. Also, consider you might be hurting someone if you are the one on the other side of this dynamic, even if they say they are okay with it. Sure, they can also end it, but let's not be in the business of hurting someone for your own benefit.

Friends with benefits (FWBs) are more defined, and is typically a situation in which both people agree that they like each other and are having sex, but that it won't be anything more. A "fuck buddy" is also that, although there might be less of a friendship component. Again, as long as people are in agreement on the structure, it's fine (until it isn't, which is discussed in the next chapter).

NON-MONOGAMY

A lot of people are exploring consensual/ethical non-monogamy (CNM/ENM) these days. There are several books on this topic (see list in the back), so I won't spend too much time on it here. There are apps and websites that are specific for it (Feeld, Swingerlifestyle (SLS), to name a few). Essentially, CNM can look many different ways, but it involves some form of open, explicit, and agreed upon non-monogamy. It is NOT dating other people and not being transparent about it. That might mean the "primary" partners date other people independently, or it might mean that they only do things as a couple (i.e. have group sex, go to sex parties, etc.), and many arrangements in between.

People might identify as "solo poly," where they are not looking for a main partner but instead have multiple ongoing significant relationships. It all depends on what you are looking for! And no shame. The main message is the same: just make sure you are on the same page with this. I've seen several successful examples of non-monogamous relationships, but it takes work (like all romantic relationships do).

There are many healthy reasons for non-monogamy, and many unhealthy ones too. The CNM couples I see in my office tend to be less on the healthy side, but that's because they clearly need help! That doesn't mean it is not a viable arrangement. Also, please do not claim being non-monogamous if you are just dating around but ultimately want to find a monogamous partner. Non-monogamy is much deeper than that, so do not use it as a reason not to commit if that is ultimately what you are looking for, but you just don't want to commit to that person.

TL;DR

- NRE is real and awesome and can be dangerous.
- Don't make major life decisions during NRE.
- Compatibility is paramount and will outlast NRE (or it won't).
- Have difficult conversations! This includes both defining the relationship, discussing dealbreakers, etc.
- There are situationships, friends with benefits, "fuck buddies", etc. The only wrong way is if you don't openly discuss it.
- There are alternatives to monogamy; again, just talk about it and be on the same page if that is something you are considering.
- Don't use non-monogamy as an excuse for lack of commitment.

HOMEWORK

- ☐ Introspect about compatibility in general. Think about this regarding your ex-wife and past partners. If you are dating someone now, think about the various dimensions of compatibility you have with them.

☐ Think about the type of person you would be most compatible with. Maybe jot it down. What are the important areas of compatibility for YOU? Perhaps discuss it with a therapist. This does not make you "too picky." This is just for your own introspection. No one is perfect, of course, but this can help you think through your priorities.

CHAPTER 15

BREAKING UP DONE RIGHT

How to End Things with Respect and Care

"I'm sorry. I can't. Don't hate me." —FAMOUSLY WRITTEN BY JACK BERGER ON A POST-IT

"All I'm saying is that there really is no good way to break up with someone, is there?" —JACK BERGER'S FRIEND

"Well, it's funny you should mention that, Billy, because actually there is. You can have the guts and the courtesy to tell a woman to her face that you no longer wanna see her. Call me crazy, but I think that you can make a point of ending your relationship in a manner that does not include an e-mail, a doorman, or a missing person's report. I think you can all get over the fear of looking like the bad guy and actually have the 'uncomfortable breakup conversation' because here's what. Avoiding that is what makes you the bad guy! And just so you know, Alan. [Andrew.] Most women aren't angry irrational psychos. We just want an ending to a relationship that is thoughtful and decent and honors what we had together. So my point, Billy, is this, there is a good way to break up with someone and it DOESN'T INCLUDE A POST-IT!" —CARRIE

G reat scene. I mean, they all are. In this one, Carrie runs into Jack Berger's friend in a club after Berger had just broken up with her on a post-it (after a break where he had said he needed space, then came back and said he wanted to make it work). She tells his friend this, and he does not react shocked as Carrie expects, and goes on to say there is no good way to break up with someone. He says that women say they are okay with being broken up with, but then they "just freak." Carrie goes on with the above monologue about how there is indeed a good way to break up with someone. I completely agree, and here it is!

In this chapter, I discuss the art of the breakup. I discuss how you might know when it is NOT working, and how to end the relationship in a mature and respectful way. I discuss a lot of "don'ts" when it comes to breakups as well.

HOW DO YOU KNOW WHEN IT ISN'T WORKING?

I discussed compatibility in depth in the last chapter. Though it is crucial for a serious relationship, it is definitely not crucial for breaking up. What I mean by this is: someone can be quite compatible with you "on paper," but this does not mean the relationship will (or should) work.

I've seen many clients and friends stay in relationships they know in their gut is not working. Of course, there are many reasons for this. This is something to explore in therapy. I had a client who, week after week, we discussed whether or not he should end his nine year relationship with his girlfriend whom he had not had sex with in seven of those years. He had googled "should I break up with my girlfriend?" several times. When it's come to googling, the answer is clearly yes.

Here are some questions to think about that might help you figure out if it isn't working:

- Do you miss her when she isn't around?

- Do you look forward to seeing her?

- Are you attracted to her?

- When you think about your future, is she in it?

- Do you look forward to talking about her with friends and family?

- Do you think about her when you are making plans? Are you excited to include her?

- Do you want to plan things (i.e. birthday celebrations, work promotions) FOR her?

- Are you excited to buy gifts for her?

- Are you excited to do things in her love language, even if it isn't yours?

- Do you like having sex with her?

- Do you still get turned on by her?

- Do you still find her sexy?

- Do you want to tell her what is going on in your life? The good and the bad?

- What does your gut say?

- Do you need to make a pro/con list?

HOW TO END IT

If the answers to most of the above questions is "no" (except the pro/con list and the gut question), it might be time to consider ending it. Most of those questions come down to envisioning a life with someone. If you can't see it easily, this is very important information.

It's not nice to string someone along. Don't be Jack Berger (post-it reference above). It's okay to communicate a break up/ending things in the same manner in which you have been communicating all along, BUT it sort of does depend on the stage of the relationship. If you are early on in the "relationship" and you text a lot and don't talk on the phone, it's okay to send a text. Especially if it is after a few dates (something along the lines of: "I've had a good time getting to know you, but I'm just not feeling the connection I'm looking for").

In an earlier chapter, I have a similar script on how to end things after one date if you get the sense she is interested in seeing you again and you are not. If you are more serious, a call or an in-person conversation is probably warranted. You can also use voice memos, if you have been doing this regularly. It's 2024! I've sat with clients in sessions while they have crafted texts or left voice memos. This works well because you can convey tone, explain things, etc., without putting someone on the spot to answer right away.

Here's the thing about breaking up. It really should not come as a surprise to either person. You should be communicating openly all along about how things are going and the things you are concerned about. At some point, it becomes clear that the things you are worried about are going to be dealbreakers. I'm guessing there were things in your marriage that you were not happy about (duh), and you didn't talk about it. Remember, this is your chance for something different and better!

The more you can talk about the things that are on your mind, the more authentic and happier you will be! You can be honest that you don't see a future with someone. You might hurt them (this is ok! It is inevitable. You are allowed to disappoint people; you are human. By nature of being human, you will disappoint), but you will hurt them much more down the line if you continue seeing them, knowing it is not forever. By prolonging a breakup, you are also preventing yourself from finding the person who IS a fit.

I've counseled many men, often avoidant attachment men, who believe they are sparing women's feelings by continuing to date them. You aren't. You are just leading them on. When you do things like: make plans, communicate with them often, have sex with them, and all the while you don't see a future with them, you are still leading them on. I have also heard many male clients say some version of "I'm honest with her that I don't want anything serious, so isn't that enough?" No, not if you are still doing the things I just listed. This is still leading her on. Yes, it is also on her to listen to and internalize what you are saying and make the best decision for her, but you are the one I am writing to.

Please don't keep dating someone you are lukewarm about until someone more compatible comes along (or someone who you are more attracted to). This is hurtful and also hurts you ultimately. Ending things creates the space for you to meet someone more compatible.

Also, it's important to learn to be on your own, especially after a long marriage. You'll attract more securely attached women if you yourself are securely attached, and the only way to learn that is to be okay on your own! Of course, this doesn't mean that you don't want to date at all, it's perfectly fine to want to date and have sex. But being okay with handling rejection and rejecting people if you don't see a future is key to secure attachment.

When breaking up with someone, you can say things like: "This just isn't working for me anymore, I'm sorry," "I don't see a future here," "I really care about you, but I don't see this working out in the long term," and so on. I can't provide an exact script for each situation of course, but those are general suggestions.

CUSHIONING/MONKEY-BARRING

Ok, this might be a good place to pause and explain the terms "cushioning" and "monkey-barring." Both of these terms essentially describe the practice of keeping (or creating) other irons in the fire with relationships and sex (actually, typically sex) in case the person you are focused on doesn't work out.

"Cushioning" is a reference to basically a soft landing after a breakup, to cushion the blow of being single, so you aren't actually single. "Monkey-barring" is a similar thing, where you are grabbing on to someone else before you let the previous partner go.

I have had many clients—both men and women—who do this. They generally have anxious attachment and are afraid to be alone, but they also are avoidant with committing to one person and seeing it through without a "safety net."

Think about how you might feel in that situation if you are any of those other parties. If you are a woman who is being kept as an option in case someone falls through, this does not feel good. The same goes for putting feelers out for other options before you end things with someone. Examples of these include: getting back on the apps before you've officially ended things with someone, continuing to talk/text/flirt/send pics etc., to someone you had a connection with while you are in a relationship with someone else, and not disclosing your relationship status to someone you are talking to. This is all misleading and manipulative. It is giving the (false) impression that you are available, and unless/until you have explicitly ended it with someone, you are not. It also makes the woman you are currently seeing feel disposable, as though you can just quickly move on.

So, use some of the tools in this book, and seek out therapy and/or additional help to be able to handle the feelings of distress after a breakup, so that you can fully end things with someone if it isn't working before moving on to someone else.

ENDING A "SITUATIONSHIP"

In some ways this can be harder than ending a defined relationship, because it is undefined. Sometimes these end because one person wants more from the other person, or one person wants more in general but not from them. Whatever the relationship is, it really is important to end it when you realize it isn't working for you anymore. Just say something like, "I've enjoyed spending time with you, but I don't think this is what I am looking for anymore."

Don't ghost (meaning don't ignore messages/requests to hang out), especially when you have been sleeping with someone. If they reach out and you aren't interested, say that. It can be harder to end a relationship where you are having sex, but if you don't see a future with someone, you are wasting both of your time (if one or both of you are really looking for something serious). If you've met someone else, it's okay to be honest about that too. Women appreciate honesty, directness, and integrity. Women can handle it!

COMMUNICATION AFTER BREAKUPS

You can do what feels right regarding communication after breaking up, but I generally find that it is healthiest in most instances to go "no-contact," at least for a period of time. This is helpful because, although it is tough and you might miss the person, the clear boundaries of no contact make it easier to move forward. Whatever reason you guys didn't work out still stands, and often it is more painful for one or both people if the contact continues. You can create more mental space for other things to come your way by going no-contact.

A note on blocking

This is controversial, but I don't think it should be. I've spent a lot of time on this topic in my sessions. Most men seem to think this step is dramatic and unnecessary. Some women are fairly quick to block. I'm a proponent of blocking if a.) you CAN (meaning you don't have to stay connected for things like co-parenting, and b.) as discussed above, someone is not bringing safety and positivity into your life.

What are some signs that blocking someone might be a good idea? Certainly, if there have been threats and you are worried for your safety (though let's be honest, this is much more applicable to women even though dramatic men will sometimes identify that this is the case). Short of that, it really is just that you don't NEED to know if she is trying to contact you.

Why would you put yourself in a position to be hurt more? Something to think about.

Knowing that someone can't get in touch with you can be very freeing. It doesn't mean there is ill-will. This is important. It just means it isn't necessary. You don't have to think someone is a bad or dangerous person in order to block them, and you are not a bad person for doing so. Give yourself permission to de-clutter your emotional life.

COPING WITH A BREAK-UP

In some ways, this whole book is about coping with a breakup, so all my advice about developing your sense-of-self of course still stands, but here I am not talking about your ex-wife, I am talking about relationships or situationships or whatever you want to call them after/during your divorce. Some of the advice is the same, like talk to a therapist if it is helpful. Keep busy. Healthy coping (exercise, hobbies, friends, media, etc.).

Don't go back through the roster. There is nothing worse than someone coming out of the woodwork long after having ended things. Look forward, not backward. Be in the discomfort. Refer to chapter one about feeling your emotions. Diving into work and/or a creative endeavor can give a huge sense of pride and accomplishment, especially if you are feeling out of control in another area of your life. Sometimes, relationships after your divorce (and subsequent breakups) can be more emotionally difficult than the ending of your marriage. This depends on the situation, level of emotional involvement, seriousness, etc.

I just want to validate and normalize the possible intensity of these post-divorce relationships, even if they don't seem as significant by comparison. What is a four-month relationship compared to a decade of marriage; one might ask. However, and hopefully you've learned this so far... don't discount your feelings. You may have felt a very strong connection, had hope for the future, felt seen/heard in a way you had not during your marriage, felt confident/attractive, been having great sex, etc. All those things matter and can of course contribute to sadness you might feel when it ends. Things also don't have to be so clearly defined to be painful when they end. Situationships, unavailable partners, etc., can all be very emotionally taxing, and an "official status" doesn't negate the feelings that might be involved.

Breaking up with someone and not "cushioning" or "monkey-barring" will likely involve a period of time not having sex. If you are a high sex drive person, this might be difficult. Just remember, horniness won't kill you. You can always take care of yourself.

I understand sex is important (I've clearly spent a lot of time discussing it in this book), but not having sex is an inevitable part of being single/personal growth. Remember, straightforward casual connections/friends-with-benefits are fine as long as you are honest, but just be aware that sometimes no sex is better than complicated sexual situations where people are unhappy/unfulfilled.

FRIENDSHIP WITH EXES

I do believe it is possible to be friends with an ex, but it takes some time and distance and it depends on the relationship. I think it is important to think about the motivation behind the friendship. I also think the likelihood of a successful friendship declines the longer you date, because things get more serious and generally more feelings are involved. This is a good place to evaluate if the motivation is self-serving and who the friendship benefits.

Also, keep in mind that things might change over time and a friendship might serve both people at one point but not forever. I have friends and clients who have remained friends with people they have had relationships with, met new people through them, found new interests/hobbies, etc., but it has to happen organically and feel right for both people. This generally means that both people are truly okay with the relationship being platonic, and one person is not secretly wishing there would be more, at least not to the point where it is emotionally harmful to themselves.

Another element to consider is if you would continue to be friends with your ex if one or both of you met someone else; this is a good litmus test for authentic friendship—if you could really be happy for them and vice versa. If not, then this might not be a friendship that is sincere.

CONTACT WITH YOUR EX-WIFE

This is a slightly different category and will be covered more in-depth in the next chapter. Of course, if you have kids and you share custody, you don't have an option to not remain in contact. If you don't have to coparent, it might be helpful to think about no-contact with your ex-wife. Maybe that is already happening, or maybe she is the driver of no-contact. This is the same principle as going no-contact with any ex, though you might feel as though it is more loaded if you were married.

You may feel like you "should" wish her a happy birthday or wish her well on a holiday, but think about WHY. This comes back to values. What purpose does this serve? Does she add something to your life? Is it something you can't get from other meaningful relationships? How does contact with her make you feel? If you see her, how does THAT make you feel? If it brings up bad feelings, pay attention to this. Life is too short to stay connected to people who make you feel bad (unless you have to).

Is one of the reasons why you are wanting to stay connected so you can feel good about how things ended? This is sometimes the case, although sometimes people don't really realize it. Introspect about this. This would mean it would be more about you and your self-image (*I'm awesome, I stay friends with all my exes!*), than it is about what the actual relationship is doing for you.

Sometimes, there are mutual friends, events you both want to be at, etc., and it is difficult to disentangle. There are good reasons to keep friends and attend events, but there are also good reasons not to.

The point is, be intentional about whatever you choose; don't fall into a trap of "shoulds." Weigh the pros and cons, picture yourself in the scenario. It's okay not to attend a wedding because you don't want to see your ex. You are protecting yourself. It's also okay to go! Like I said, no one-size-fits-all approach. This, of course, can all apply to any ex by the way.

TL;DR

- Remember this phrase: "I've really enjoyed getting to know you, but I don't think we have the romantic connection I am looking for."

- Once you know you don't see a future, end it. Don't string along.
- Saying one thing in the name of honesty and acting differently can still be stringing along.
- Be honest and direct. Honesty is appreciated; women can handle it.
- Consider going no-contact, depending on the circumstances.
- Blocking is cool, do it if you want. You aren't a bad person.
- Think carefully about the role that feels right for your ex to play in your life. There is no one-size-fits-all approach.

HOMEWORK

- ☐ Consider your values and how your romantic relationships are or are not in line with your values.
- ☐ If you are led to a decision from this introspection, take action!

SO, YOUR WIFE LEFT YOU... NOW WHAT?

CHAPTER 16

ALL THINGS EX-WIFE, PARENTING, AND CO-PARENTING
Managing Life After Divorce

"I'm not exactly thrilled our baby is having sex yet, but I sure am glad he's using protection" —MIRANDA

Miranda says this when she finds condoms in the diaper bag that she shares with Steve, the father of her baby (who is dating someone else), when Steve drops off the baby. Miranda and Steve were not married and subsequently divorced, but they have a child together that they share, so I thought this was still relevant. Co-parenting is incredibly tricky. This chapter will discuss coparenting and kids. I will go over how to connect with your kids, what is important about parenting during this time, how to talk to your kids about the divorce, custody, kid time, kid-free time, coparenting (both in a reflective sense and moving forward), and all things involving dating and kids. This is of course a complicated topic, on which there are many books, so this is all "bite-size" advice. Of course you can skip this if you don't have kids, though why not stick with it if you've come this far!

PARENTING

This is a super critical time for excellent parenting, if there ever was a time for it. Obviously, no parent is perfect, but it is crucial right now that you are a secure and stable base for your kids. This is true regardless of how old your kids are. If they are in the home still, hands-on parenting is going to be much more relevant than if they are older. However, even with older/ adult kids, how you "parent" during this time is crucial. You need to be available to them, in many senses of the word. Dr. Samantha Rodman Whiten wrote a book called *How To Talk to Your Kids About Your Divorce*, which I definitely recommend if you want more in-depth coverage of the topic, including different age ranges. This chapter will not go into as much detail, but will provide an overview regarding what to say and how to connect with your kids during this time. Whether you are reading this early on in your separation, or it's been awhile, it's never too late to reconnect with your kids and prioritize the relationship. The single best thing you can do for your kiddos during this time is to be as loving, stable, and CALM as you can be. This means doing what you need to do for your own mental health—being as amicable with your coparent as possible, not fighting over everything (truly, the soccer schedule matters so much less than being a calm presence for them), increasing the self- care (exercise, therapy, etc.), and thinking carefully about your love life.

This is a lifechanging event for them, of course. They are having a lot of emotions around your divorce (regardless of age), and they NEED YOU to be able to handle those emotions. Obviously, the way you handle it and the issues that arise post/ during divorce will vary widely depending on your kids age, your custody arrangement, etc.

Remember the first chapter on how emotions serve a purpose and are hardwired into us? These are excellent principles to remember when it comes to your kids. The majority of men reading this will likely have some physical and legal custody these days (if your kids are younger than 18), and questions from them are inevitable. They might make you uncomfortable; they might make you feel bad or guilty. These are feelings to process with a therapist! But, the worst thing to do is shut down these conversations. Let them know that you are there for them and are receptive to their questions and can handle their emotions. If you are noticing significant behavior changes, problems in school, or if their teachers are saying something, consider finding them a good therapist to help them explore their feelings about everything. However, it bears repeating that the single best thing you can do for them is taking care of yourself and your own emotions. Consider your own therapy even before theirs, because if you are having a hard time dealing with their emotions/behaviors, that is on YOU.

HOW TO TALK TO YOUR KIDS ABOUT THE DIVORCE

This is another good place to pause and think about the messages you received growing up about emotions. Use the principles discussed in chapter one to talk to your kids and sit with their emotions. Validate them. They are allowed to be angry, sad, scared, uncertain, etc. Say things like, "it's ok to be sad." Let them express themselves. They need to be able to count on you. They will likely have questions, and it's really important to be direct and straightforward with them. Kids want to hear the truth about things; they feel safe that way. If you are not confident about your answers, they will feel less secure. If you are reading this, you are likely at the stage where you have already told them about the divorce, so I'm going to focus on things that might continue to come up throughout the process.

Here are some questions that might come up and some ways to address them (remember, if you want more details, read Dr. Rodman's book). Of course, the biggest question from kids is why did you get divorced. Dr. Rodman discusses using the phrase, "we got divorced because we don't love each other the way married people should." This phrasing mostly applies to younger kids, but the same sentiment can be applied to older kids as well. Because that is the truth! Same answer if they ask if you still love their mom. "Not like married people should." This answer accomplishes a few important things: One, it's straightforward. If you answer "yes" to the question of if you love their mom, they will wonder why you are not still married. It is confusing. Kids don't do well with confusion or uncertainty. They would rather know the information, even if it is hard. This is also the case for other difficult topics like death, sex, current events, etc. You need to be the confident base. Use the word "divorced," and don't treat it like it's a bad word. This answer also sends the message that married people should love each other in a way that you and their mom didn't, which is true! This is the whole reason why this is an opportunity for you. You now have the opportunity to find a new love and model that relationship for your kids. Even if that doesn't happen, at least they are not seeing a loveless marriage or worse, a high-conflict one anymore.

Do not say, "but we still love you and will always love you" unless you are explicitly asked this question (i.e. if you still love them). Kids are suggestible. This will plant a seed of doubt in their mind that you don't love them, and you definitely do not want to do that. If they say they miss their mom, you can empathize with them, but do not say you do too (even if this is the case). If they tell you they miss their mom, tell them you are glad they told you! You want your kids to tell you how they feel, and you always want to send the message that you can handle their feelings. If they tell you this, this is a great thing and you should reinforce it. You want to be a safe space where they can talk about their mom! If you say you miss her too, this could confuse them. If you miss them, why aren't you with them? If they ask you if you miss them, your answer might depend on a few things. You can say "I don't miss her the way married people should miss each other." This sounds a bit cold, I know, but you are really doing your kids a favor by drawing very clear boundaries around the relationship and teaching them what healthy romantic and not romantic relationships should look like! If you do miss her, you can say something like, "I miss some things about the relationship." If they ask you questions about your marriage, the history, etc., definitely answer them honestly. Your kids want you to be real with them, just don't treat them like friends (or worse, therapists!). Being straightforward also teaches kids that relationships are complicated and nuanced, which they are! If you don't miss her at all and there is a lot of animosity, say the first thing. More on how to talk about your coparent in the next section.

How to talk about your coparent? Never talk poorly about them. It seems obvious, but there are many ways to convey negative sentiments about your coparent. You can be outright mean, or you can be passive-aggressive. Don't do either. This is toxic and will have lifelong effects for your kids. Don't suggest that they are responsible for the divorce, either, even if this is the case. They are the one that maybe decided to leave, but both people are responsible for the deterioration of the marriage. This can cause parental alienation, as your kids might align with you and against their mom, and you don't actually want that. You want what is best for them, which is a close and loving relationship with both their parents. It also might backfire and they might get defensive of her, which can result in alienating them from YOU. Remember this next point, it is almost as important as oral sex isn't foreplay. You are not only talking about your kids' mom, but you are talking to human being(s) that are genetically half of your ex-wife. So, when you talk shit about their mom, you are essentially telling them that half of them is that way too. This will take a huge toll on their self-esteem and confidence. If you build up your coparent, it will help immensely.

To that end, one VERY important thing to do, is to actually talk UP your coparent. Dr. Rodman emphasizes this point too. Try to say one good/nice thing about them every day! This will not only help them to see the positive qualities in their mom, but it will increase their own self-esteem (remember, they are half of their other parent). I know you can think of one nice thing about her to say every day to them. Talk about what she is good at, that she's smart, etc. Do NOT do this in a wistful "I miss her" kind of way, but in an enthusiastic way, like you would talk about an aunt or uncle. For instance, if your kids come home and they learned a new song they like, you can say something along the lines of, "awesome! Share that with your mom, too! She has great taste in music!" If you haven't been do-ing this, it is never too late to course correct. If you truly have a hard time thinking of anything positive to say, therapy can help. Don't bullshit this, kids are smart. It will also help YOU to think of the positive qualities in your ex; this will only help you be a better coparent, if you don't see them as an awful, terrible person. Our minds are incredibly powerful, and this is a very important reframe.

CUSTODY AND COPARENTING

Whatever your custody arrangement is, make the most of your kid time AND your kid-free time. It can be hard at first, but you'll get used to not having them all the time. Plus, if you actually look at the breakdown of time spent with your kids, it is likely that you actually will spend MORE—or at least equal—time with them now than you did when you were married, especially if you have 50/50 custody. Parents these days, especially in marriages that end in divorce, spend a ton of time tag-teaming the kids, meaning switching off parenting (on the weekends for example, when one parents takes the kids while the other does errands, or they divide and conquer with multiple kids, etc. This is not always a good approach and is often indicative of larger problems). So really, it's not actually all that different when you break down the hours, and you get to spend your kid time exactly the way you want! I'm guessing a lot of conflict in your marriage was around parenting. This is also something to discuss in therapy and think about for the future. Hardly anything is actually worth fighting over. Kids activities, clothing, snacks, schools...It wasn't worth the fight when you were married, and it certainly isn't now. It's okay (and good!) to parent differently. Your kids get exposure to different approaches, as they do in the world anyway! I discuss this more often with my clients who are women actually, who find it very difficult to accept the lack of control they have when their kids are with their dad, or even cite it as a reason to stay in a bad marriage. It truly does not matter what they pack for lunch. A peaceful home is much more important.

You now have the freedom to parent the way you want, within the bounds of your legal custody agreement of course. If there is animosity, and you are currently involved in a legal battle, I do encourage you to heavily weigh the pros and cons of this.

It will take a huge toll on you in many ways, and your kids will pick up on this. You simply cannot be the best parent you can be if you are involved in a legal battle. Sometimes it's worth it (for example, if your coparent is refusing medical or mental health help for your kids). I obviously don't know the particulars of your situation, but this is just generally speaking. Your kids will pick up on the stress, and this can cause anxiety, depression, behavioral issues, etc. (again depending on their age and other factors). So, make it a goal to try to be agreeable as a coparent moving forward. Practically, this can include saying things like, "Yes, good point," "I hadn't thought about that," "Sure, I can take the kids this weekend." This will really help you see your ex more positively, which will lead to being the best version of yourself! Ultimately, this is the best thing to do for your kids, of course. It is also good practice for dating moving forward. Most people like agreeable people (i.e. not difficult people!) and want to avoid stressful and toxic interactions.

When you are solo parenting, you really do have the opportunity to seriously bond with your kids in a special way. Remember, they're still your kids, so do not interact with them like they are adults. Do not talk to them about your adult problems. Do not put the emotional load on them. But, do have fun with them! Do activities they like to do, teach them stuff you like, try new things. You have the opportunity to parent the way you want to without bickering or fighting, so take advantage! Teach them the world is their oyster, like yours is. Teach them to be excited about life! As I mentioned in a previous chapter, involve them in your new home (if applicable).

On the topic of your home, please do what you can to make transitions as easy as possible for the kids. If they need two different sets of things at each house, do your best to accommodate. Have calendars showing their schedule so they can keep track themselves. Let them take the lead on what they want to take back and forth and what they want to keep at each place. Dr. Rodman also discusses using the phrase "living with mom/dad" as opposed to "staying with." This conveys that they have two homes, and they live in both of them. They are not guests. Language is important.

A note on hand-offs. Transitions between homes can be tough, so please try to make these as seamless as possible. Sometimes, school is the best time for transitions, where one parent drops off and the other picks up. If your kid(s) has a lot of stuff to bring back and forth, they can bring it to school if they are okay with that (check in about this. It might be too cumbersome or socially awkward, or they might not have an issue with it), or you can drop it at their coparent's house for them to make things easier (this is always your job, to make things easier for them). If you are transitioning directly between homes, please keep these brief, friendly, and do not use this as a time to argue or discuss logistics with your coparent. This transition should feel as calm and safe as it can be for the kids. Make sure they have what they need. If you are the parent handing off, express enthusiasm about their upcoming time with their mom, so as to assuage any possible (unnecessary) guilt they might feel "leaving" you. You don't want them to worry about you. That isn't their job. If you are overly emotional about them leaving, they might worry about how you are doing when you aren't with them. Of course, you can be warm, however. You can say things like, "I had a great time with you! I love you! Have the best time with your mom, see you on Friday!"

When you are receiving them, make sure your home is ready for them, and you are emotionally ready for them. Do not pepper them with questions immediately when they return. You can express interest in wanting to hear about their time, but often the transitions are hard and they need a minute to settle in. You might be able to relate: if you were coming back from a work trip - tired, trying to get organized, etc., you would likely not want an interrogation. Remember, calm environment. Do not try to get information from the kids about their other home; they can sense this. Just be warm and inviting and calm. They will share and then you can follow-up.

When you don't have your kids, enjoy your kid-free time! If you share custody, your kids are with their other parent, not a babysitter, so try to let the guilt go, if you feel any. They are loved and cared for, so you can enjoy your time! It gets easier. If you have not watched *Fleishman is in Trouble* on Hulu, do so immediately. Seriously. It is incredibly relatable in a tough yet really beautiful way. Claire Danes and Jesse Eisenberg play a well-off divorcing couple in New York with school-aged kids. There is an excellent scene of Jesse Eisenberg's first kid-free weekend (this is not a spoiler) in his new apartment, eating Chinese food on a bean bag chair and swiping on Tinder. It's the moment that he realizes he is actually attractive to women, and it is pretty epic to watch. But, don't just sit around swiping on Tinder in your kid-free time. Refer back to my earlier chapter about things to focus on. You will come to appreciate the time. Also, share what you do with your kids when they come back to you. It is important for them to know you have a life! Which, hopefully, you do! They should know you are active and using the time, otherwise they might worry about you (especially if you are single). Involve them in your life. Take pictures and show them when they get back. Bring them souvenirs if you travel, tell them stories, etc. Remember, you are modeling that adulthood is fun (even if you yourself did not get that model)!

HOLIDAYS, BIRTHDAYS, ETC.

This is a tough one because it can bring up a lot. It could be really difficult not to have certain holidays with your kids. Of course, stick to a custody agreement if you have one already, but I encourage you to think outside the box with all this. Try to move away from a rigid definition of "fairness" and think about what is best for your kids. You can celebrate your kids' birthdays on a different day. You can "celebrate" silly holidays like National Ice Cream day, or even make up your own! Making your own traditions will be even more special to your kids as they grow up. I encourage you to see things from their perspective and try to make the holidays as stress-free for them as possible. This might involve giving up a holiday that you'd like to have with them in order to make things relaxed for them. This is a huge benefit to them. You are truly doing the best thing for them. I've had clients split Christmas, for example, as opposed to rotating years, because both parents want some part of the holiday. This can often take away from the joys of the holiday for the kids, and creates a lot of anxiety for them. They might be spending the holiday anticipating the transition, rather than enjoying the time. The same goes for their birthdays. I've had clients who insist on throwing their kids a birthday party even though their coparent is also throwing them a birthday party. I encourage them to think about the hardship this could cause for the kids: it is awkward to invite friends to two different parties, or have to pick which friends to have at which party. You should be making things easier for your kids, not harder. If their mom is throwing them a party, consider celebrating their birthday another way, like a special activity or a "yes day" (one of these popular things on social media where you say yes to everything your kids want that day). Please keep all this in mind and try to do right by them. In this context, "right" means the least amount of chaos possible for them, regardless of what might be "fair" in terms of time split, etc. When things are stressful for the kids, they will remember that more than the holiday itself.

If you are on your own for a special holiday, I know this can be tough. Get together with friends or your own family if that feels fulfilling to you. Ask other people to get together. Develop your own ways of celebrating. Do something for you. Look at the silver linings: possibly fewer obligations. Refer to chapter one—be in your feels. But also look at the freedom/opportunities. I have many clients who have discovered the joys of ordering in on Thanksgiving and not having to stress over family, in-laws, etc. I have a client who used to hate the week between Christmas and New Years because he doesn't have his kids and he misses them, and now he loves the time.

A RELATED NOTE

When you are only with your kid half the time, it might be hard not to put pressure on that time to be amazing. Try not to do "divorced parent math," where you get stuck on only having them X amount of time (for example, only 5 weekends in the summer), so you have to make the most of all the time. Remember, you are still parenting—with all its ups and downs. Not everything will be special and incredible because it is the only warm summer beach day, sometimes your kids might still have a meltdown. This is normal; try not to let that ruin your time. On that note, please do not prevent them from doing normal kid activities (extracurriculars, playdates, sleepovers, trips, etc.) because your time is limited and it "takes away" your time. This is unfair to them and takes away typical childhood experiences. A divorce is hard enough on them (even a non-conflictual one), so don't let them miss out. Think about what they would be doing if you were still in a household with married parents, and let them do that. @MichelleDempsy on Instagram discusses divorce coparenting in a really lovely way, and talks about this.

MOTHER'S DAY/FATHER'S DAY

This deserves its own paragraph because these holidays can be very difficult post-divorce. I think it is really important to acknowledge the holiday and help your kids celebrate their mom. No matter what the status is with you, she will always be their mother, and it is important to celebrate and acknowledge that. It is also important to teach your kids to do the same! As you know, us parents work hard! James Sexton also discusses the importance of this. He is himself divorced, and he talks about how he helps his kids get their mom cards on Mother's Day. Even if she does not do it for Father's Day (and she should), be the mature person here and do the right thing. I know my clients in these situations very much appreciate it.

COMMUNICATION WITH YOUR CO-PARENT

I touched on this above, but I really can't stress enough to try to be as agreeable as you can. I'm sure there are a lot of lingering feelings still, and that is all okay. But please try to deal with those difficult feelings in a way that minimizes the impact on your kids and your co-parent relationship. Try to be flexible where you can be, say hi and be polite/kind when you see each other. Keep the boundaries of the co-parent relationship, but you can do this in a way that is respectful and kind.

On the flip side, be mindful of your own mental health, and if something is really too much for you, it's fine to sit it out (for example, a mutual friend's party). As I've said before, the best thing to do as a parent is take care of yourself. If you are doing that, you should be able to interact with your co-parent in a reasonable way. If you find yourself getting triggered easily, short-tempered, irritable, etc., you might want to check in with yourself.

You can control your reactions to things. You can't control your co-parent, but you can reframe things in your mind and control your response. You can tell yourself things like, *she is doing her best, she loves her kids, she is a great mom, this is hard for her too.* That last one is especially important because it helps to cultivate empathy.

Divorce is hard for everyone, even the person that initiated it. Your co-parent is struggling with parenting as well, navigating interactions with you, trying to make the best decisions for the kids, and the like. Again, if you are having trouble with all this, it is a great topic for therapy.

DATING WITH KIDS

Obviously a lot of this book is on this topic, but in terms of the relevance here: Your kids are the priority and need your love and attention. Your kid-free time is for dating. If you have full custody, then you will probably need babysitters. But if you have 50/50 (whatever the split is), I encourage you to limit the time you date to when you don't have your kids, and give them your full attention when you do. Dating after divorce can be a lot of things: Fun, exciting, sexy, novel, difficult, stressful, anxiety provoking, sad, complicated, etc. It is your responsibility to be as mentally healthy as you can for your kids, so try to focus on people that facilitate that, as opposed to contributing to instability. Of course, we all learn as we go and everything is an experience, but just something to keep in mind.

When to introduce the kids to a new partner

This also of course depends on your kids age, your unique situation, etc. As a general principle, do not introduce your kids to anyone until it is serious in your mind. In this context, this means someone you have been seeing for long enough that you can picture a future with them. You might be legally bound by your divorce agreement to wait a certain period of time, to have your coparent meet your partner first or at least discuss it with them, or any number of arrangements. Obviously, follow this agreement. If you are not legally bound to a specific scenario, it is still important to make sure it's someone who you foresee sticking around. This likely won't happen for a good bit after your divorce, unless you are anxiously attached in which case you probably think you are "ready" sooner than you are. Again... Therapist.

Of course, it is important for a prospective partner to get along with your kids, and you probably want to see how they interact, so don't wait TOO long either, but hopefully, you would know them well enough to be able to anticipate how they would be with your kids. If you are concerned about this, this could be a red flag and do not ignore it. Kids get attached, but it is also okay if you introduce them to someone and it doesn't work out. Obviously, that happens. It would be like if a friend of yours moved away. This happens and it's not the end of the world for kids to know that. Just don't introduce them to flings if you know it is going to be a fling.

If you have older kids (preteens and beyond), you can talk to them about your dating life, at an age-appropriate level. You can tell them you are seeing someone and you'd like for them to meet at some point, but don't force it. Let them see that you are happy and in the best case scenario, they will ask to meet them.

Meeting someone else's kid(s):

Of course if you are dating someone with kids, the question will arise regarding you meeting them. Go with your gut on this too. Do not feign enthusiasm about meeting kids if you are not prepared to do it. It has to be genuine excitement for meeting them. Talk about your feelings around all of it and decide together when it feels right.

When either of you meet each other's kids, do so in a neutral place. Dr. Rodman suggests a low-pressure activity, like bowling or the zoo (something age-appropriate); this provides something else to focus on and makes it more of a casual hangout. Then, you can slowly spend more time, do more intimate things, etc., as the relationship and the trust builds.

As is the case with everything, you will learn as you go. If you have already introduced or met kids and it didn't work out, it's okay! Lessons to learn. Wait until it FEELS right, and if it doesn't, it is usually not.

SETTING AN EXAMPLE FOR A LOVING RELATIONSHIP

Remember, you—eventually—have an amazing opportunity here to set an example for a loving relationship with a new partner. Just like your family of origin was the blueprint for romantic relationships for you, your relationship is the blueprint for your kids. Kids should see adults in romantic relationships be loving, warm, physically and verbally affectionate with each other, have fun together, laugh, flirt, compliment each other, support each other, and communicate issues/resolve conflict in a healthy way. When modeling a romantic relationship, ask yourself if you would want your kids to have the relationship that you have. I assume, regarding your ex, the answer is "no!" Duh. So, here is the opportunity!

A word on physical affection in front of your kids. Do it. Don't be inappropriate, obviously (for example, don't stick your hands down each other's pants around your kids), but your kids should see you kiss, hug, hold hands, massage each other, etc. They should know that physical affection is an important part of a healthy romantic relationship, and they learn this from you! Most of my adult clients who had healthy marriages modeled (granted, there aren't many because most of those don't come to therapy), knew that their parents had sex! In a good way. Model the sex positivity that you likely did not have.

If you don't have a partner to do this with, all good! Don't rush into anything for the sake of setting this example; it will backfire. Take your time and make sure that it's right, so that when you do have it, it's the right example! It's also great for kids to see independent single parents doing things on their own and having a life of their own.

STEP-PARENTING AND BLENDED FAMILIES

I won't spend too much time here because it might be pretty far in the future, but I do want to address blending families/becoming a step-parent. It can be complicated, but can also be a wonderful thing! It takes time and lots of empathy on everyone's part to be able to navigate these complicated dynamics. Family therapy can help with the bumps in the road, if there are any.

Your role as a step-parent is to be a supportive and loving adult presence in the step-kid's lives. If they have a dad in the picture, great! They don't need another one, and that relationship needs to be respected, just like you would want yours to be if your ex-wife got remarried and your kids had a stepdad. Do not be the disciplinarian; let mom do that. Take her lead when it comes to her kids. Support HER while she supports the kids.

There is a lot of rhetoric (especially in the "manosphere") about how single moms are just looking for a dad for their kids. If you are reading this book, hopefully you are interested in dating and partnering with women for whom this could not be farther from the truth. Most successful smart women have the mom thing down; they just want a partner (if that's what they are looking for). So don't believe that, and let her take the lead on the parenting. If you get the sense that she is looking for something you are not prepared to give, please gracefully exit the situation.

Also, of course you are free to not date women with kids! Though I find that most men with kids see that as a bonus because you have parenting in common, but certainly not everyone sees it that way. There are of course more complications with a blended family, and there are pros (like easier logistics) to keeping it simple.

There is not a one-size-fits-all approach to step/blended families, so I encourage you to keep these principles in mind. Hopefully, you and your partner are on the same page about this, which of course speaks to my points mentioned throughout this book about compatibility. Someone who has the same values, visions, priorities as you. Don't let things get this far if that is not the case (refer to previous chapter).

TL;DR

- The most important thing for kids is a loving, supportive, CALM environment.

- Listen to your kids and talk about their emotions; validate.

- Find them a therapist if that would be helpful, but perhaps more importantly, learn how to manage your own emotional responses to them.

- Don't put too much pressure on your time; parenting is still parenting. Let them do normal kid things even if it takes away from your time.

- You have the opportunity to model living a full and exciting life! Don't teach your kids that being an adult sucks.

- Also enjoy your kid-free time. Engage in valued activities here too. Tell your kids about what you do with the time.

- Almost nothing is worth a fight with your ex about your kids; this takes a huge toll on their well-being and mental health. Let that shit go.

- Language around your divorce is important.

- If you are doing direct handoffs, keep them short and friendly. Make sure your kid(s) have everything they need. Be enthusiastic about sending them off to their co-parent.

- Don't talk shit, in fact do the opposite. Talk up your coparent! Say something nice on a DAILY basis.

- Wait to introduce kids to a partner until it feels like you can see a future.

- You have the opportunity to model a loving relationship; don't take it lightly.
- Don't worry about not being partnered. Take your time. You can model independence and waiting for the right fit.
- Step-parenting and blending families can be a wonderful thing, but requires care and caution.

HOMEWORK

- ☐ Talk to your kids about their feelings. Let them know you are there for them and want to hear what they have to say.
- ☐ Say one nice thing about your coparent daily.
- ☐ Date people who bring stability, not instability (Lol on this as a homework assignment. So easy, right??).
- ☐ Talk to your kids more about your kid-free activities.
- ☐ As always, introspect about all this!

CONCLUSION

"The most exciting, challenging, and significant relationship of all is the one you have with yourself. And if you find someone to love the you that you love, well, that's just fabulous." —CARRIE BRADSHAW

Y ou made it! Thanks for sticking with me, especially through all my *Sex and the City* quotes. This might be the most overused one from the series, but it is actually so true. I had to end with this one because in many ways this whole book is about empowering you to be your best self! This is the last voiceover of the entire series, where Big (aka John) calls her and says he is officially moving back to New York to be with her, after six years of back and forth. She is basically saying that you have to love yourself first. Yes! Someone else is just a bonus (a wonderful one, if it's right).

I want to recap a bit here and set the tone moving forward. I really hope some of this has been helpful in order to reframe your divorce. I hope to have given some helpful practical advice as well as some general pearls of wisdom. This advice will all not only benefit you, but the people around you including your kids.

Divorce is scary. It is unknown. Your whole life has changed. No one ever goes into a marriage planning for or wanting divorce. Please don't take my messages here as evidence that I am cavalier about divorce and the impact of it. My goal is to point out the opportunity for learning and growth that never would have happened had you stayed married. The valuable lessons come from the painful shit. It's cliché but so true.

When you think back on your marriage, try to think about the underlying pattern. The content of the argument (sex, finances, in-laws, kids) is only a symptom of the dysfunctional pattern you had. The biggest issues I have seen involve fundamental incompatibilities, insecure attachment styles/unresolved childhood issues and a lack of introspection around this, people's needs not being met (perhaps because they don't even realize it themselves, and certainly in part because of how hard it is to communicate those needs), those needs changing along with a judgment about that rather than an understanding, being judgmental and closed-minded in general, an abundance of the four horseman, and a ton of resentment with an unwillingness (or lack of skill) to discuss past ruptures and repair them. I know it is hard to own your part in things, but you will truly not be able to move on and get what you want in life (and deserve to have!) if you can't do some serious self-reflection and thinking about it.

As for moving forward, try to put some of this stuff into action. Small changes go a long way. Some personal touches to your home. Taking the stairs. Reading this book! Reaching out to a friend. Connecting with spirituality. Taking an online quiz. Self-reflection. As I said in chapter seven, this is all movement toward growth. Check out the references/recommended reading/watching/listening in the back of this book for more resources on all the topics covered here.

Based on my experience, I believe the future of relationships is changing. I think people are getting married later or not at all, and are prioritizing compatibility. This is especially true for women, who are also realizing they don't need men in their lives, financially or to feel happy and fulfilled, and thus they are raising the bar for partnerships. I believe this is a good thing because I believe it will result in the most compatible people getting married, and thus the happiest relationships. It will probably result in fewer kids, which could also be a good thing because the people who are having them will really want them. The lesson with all this is: don't settle. Get to know yourself and what you want and be discerning until you find something great! Learn to enjoy your own company. It's okay (and human) to be lonely. Sit with it. It's great to have a wonderful partner; but they have to make your already great life even better. Being partnered is not the be-all-end all anymore.

As for me, feel free to reach out and let me know your thoughts on all this. I hope to write more books and continue to build my career and my practice. I'd love to do groups, workshops, speaking engagements, etc. on these topics. It was difficult to stop writing this because things kept coming up that I wanted to add! So, more material for the next one!

Realizing the silver linings of divorce come with time and experience, truly finding your valued activities, and hindsight/reflection. During this writing process, people asked me how I found the time to do it. My answer is: we ALL can find the time to do the things that are important to us. We make choices everyday regarding how to spend our time. This reflects our values and priorities. When we are living a valued/fulfilled life (not necessarily *happy*, but fulfilled), we are our best selves. Sometimes there is only space and time for that after you are out of an unhealthy situation. If you have made it this far, even though you likely did not make the choice to leave, you have been given the opportunity for this. To get to know YOU. Take this opportunity. Own your part in things and be reflective going forward. We are all lifelong learners.

REFERENCES AND FURTHER SUGGESTED CONTENT

References and suggested reading/watching/listening are organized by chapter; some may appear more than once.

INTRODUCTION

Waldinger, R. J., & Schulz, M. (2023). *The good life: lessons from the world's longest scientific study of happiness.* First Simon & Schuster hardcover edition. New York, Simon & Schuster.

Reynolds, L. (2021). The U.S. remarriage rate, 2019: Trends and geographic variation by gender. *Family Profiles*, FP-21-18. Bowling Green, OH: National Center for Family & Marriage Research. https://doi.org/10.25035/ncfmr/fp-21-18

Divorce statistics 2024: Everything you need to know. Graziano & Flynn, P.C. (2024, August 28). https://www.grazianolaw. com/blog/divorce-statistics/#:~:text=Additionally%2C%20 most%20people%20tend%20to,alimony%2C%20and%20 child%20support%20agreements.

CHAPTER 1. SHE SAYS I'M EMOTIONLESS:
NAMING AND UNDERSTANDING YOUR EMOTIONS

Sex and the City, Season 5 episode 2, "Unoriginal Sin."

Kübler-Ross, E. (1969). *On death and dying*. The Macmillan Company.

Lenz, L. (2024). *This American Ex-Wife*. Crown.

Docter, P., & Del Carmen, C. (Directors). (2015). *Inside Out* [Film]. Disney Pixar.

Mann, K. (Director). (2024). *Inside Out 2* [Film]. Disney Pixar.

Linehan, M. (2014). *DBT Skills Training Handouts and Worksheets* (2nd ed.). Guilford Press.

CHAPTER 2. I SHOULD PROBABLY GET A LAWYER:
A BRIEF GUIDE TO THE LEGAL PROCESS

Sex and the City, Season 5 episode 6, "Critical Condition."

Wallerstein, J. S., Lewis, J. M., & Blakeslee, S. (2001). *The Unexpected Legacy of Divorce: The 25 Year Landmark Study*. Grand Central Publishing.

CHAPTER 3. OKAY, LET'S TALK THERAPY:
HOW TO FIND THE RIGHT HELP FOR YOU

Sex and the City, Season 2 episode 13, "Games People Play."

American Psychiatric Association, *DSM-5 Task Force. (2013). Diagnostic and statistical manual of mental disorders: DSM-5*™ (5th ed.). American Psychiatric Publishing, Inc..

CHAPTER 4. THERAPY 101:
WHAT IT IS AND WHY IT MATTERS

Sex and the City, Season 2 episode 13, "Games People Play."

Beck, J. S. (2021). *Cognitive behavior therapy: Basics and beyond* (3rd ed.). The Guilford Press.

Martell, C. R., Dimidjian, S., & Lewinsohn, P. M. (2010). *Behavioral activation therapy for depression: A clinician's guide.* The Guilford Press.

Hayes, S. C., Strosahl, K. D., & Wilson, K. G. (2012). *Acceptance and commitment therapy: The process and practice of mindful change* (2nd ed.). The Guilford Press.

Linehan, M. (2014). *DBT Skills Training Handouts and Worksheets* (2nd ed.). Guilford Press.

Abramowitz, J. S., Deacon, B. J., & Whiteside, S. P. H. (2019). *Exposure therapy for anxiety: Principles and practice* (2nd ed.). The Guilford Press.

Summers, R. F., & Barber, J. P. (2010). *Psychodynamic therapy: A guide to evidence-based practice.* Guilford Press.

Gottman, J. M., & Gottman, J. S. (2023). *Gottman method couple therapy.* The Guilford Press.

Johnson, 2019: *The practice of emotionally focused couple therapy: Creating connection* (3rd ed.), Routledge/Taylor & Francis Group.

Gibson, L. (2015). *Adult Children of Emotionally Immature Parents: How to Heal From Distant, Rejecting, or Self-Involved Parents.* New Harbinger Publications.

Hendrix, H., PhD, & Hunt, H. L., PhD (2019). *Getting the Love You Want: A Guide for Couples* (3rd ed.). St. Martin's Griffin.

CHAPTER 5. WHAT JUST HAPPENED?!:
A STRAIGHTFORWARD LOOK AT WHY MARRIAGES FALL APART

Sex and the City, Season 4 episode 18, "I Heart NY."

@nycdivorcelawyer

@drpsychmom

Spengler, P. M., Lee, N. A., Wiebe, S. A., & Wittenborn, A. K. (2024). A comprehensive meta-analysis on the efficacy of emotionally focused couple therapy. *Couple and Family Psychology: Research and Practice*, 13(2), 81–99. https://doi.org/10.1037/cfp0000233

Fray, M. (2016, January 25). She Divorced Me Because I Left Dishes By The Sink. *Huff Post*.

Gottman J, & Silver N (1999). *The Seven Principles for Making Marriage Work*. Crown Publishers.

(n.d.). *The Apology Language™ Quiz*. 5 Love Languages. Retrieved December 23, 2024, from https://5lovelanguages.com/quizzes/apology-language

CHAPTER 6. AM I REALLY AVOIDANT?:
THE TRUTH ABOUT ATTACHMENT STYLES AND RELATIONSHIPS

Sex and the City, Season 2 episode 12, "La Douleur Exquise!"

Levine, A., & Heller, R. (2012). *Attached: The New Science of Adult Attachment and How It Can Help You Find—and Keep—Love.* TarcherPerigee.

Johnson, S., EdD (2012). *Hold Me Tight: Seven Conversations for a Lifetime of Love.* Little, Brown Spark.

Ainsworth, M. D. S., Blehar, M. C., Waters, E., & Wall, S. (1978). Strange Situation Procedure (SSP) [Database record]

Coelen, C. (Director). (2020-). *Love is Blind* [Series]. Kinetic Content.

CHAPTER 7. I WANT TO BE MY BEST SELF:
WHAT TO WORK ON BEFORE YOU START DATING

Sex and the City, Season 1 episode 9, "Turtle and the Hare."

Aron, E. (1998). *The Highly Sensitive Person: How to Thrive When the World Overwhelms You.* Three Rivers Press.

Alcoholics Anonymous World Services (2001). *Alcoholics Anonymous: The story of how many thousands of men and women have recovered from alcoholism.* Alcoholics Anonymous World Services.

Horvath, A. T., & Yeterian, J. (2012). Smart recovery: Self-empowering, science-based addiction recovery support. *Journal of Groups in Addiction & Recovery*, 7(2-4), 102–117. https://doi.org/10.1080/1556035X.2012.705651

Lenz, L. (2024). *This American Ex-Wife.* Crown.

CHAPTER 8. SWIPE RIGHT, SWIPE LEFT:
NAVIGATING ONLINE DATING AND MEETING NEW PEOPLE

Sex and the City, Season 4 episode 1, "The Agony and the Ecstasy."

@alittlenudge

Valentine JL, Miles LW, Mella Hamblin K, Worthen Gibbons A. Dating App Facilitated Sexual Assault: A Retrospective Review of Sexual Assault Medical Forensic Examination Charts. *J Interpers Violence.* 2023 May;38(9-10):6298-6322. doi: 10.1177/08862605221130390. Epub 2022 Oct 29. PMID: 36310506.

CHI '07: Proceedings of the SIGCHI Conference on Human Factors in Computing Systems; The truth about lying in online dating profiles, pages 449 - 452

Shammas, B., & Lati, M. (2024, March 2). Are we dating the same guy? Facebook groups offer intel but upend lives. *The Washington Post.*

CHAPTER 9. THE FIRST DATE PLAYBOOK:
HOW TO MAKE A GREAT IMPRESSION

Sex and the City, Season 5 episode 3, "Luck Be an Old Lady."

@alittlenudge

(2024, May 15). The Green Flags Study. *Tinder Newsroom.*

CHAPTER 10. ORAL SEX IS NOT FOREPLAY: WHAT NO ONE TELLS YOU ABOUT SEX AND WHAT IT IS REALLY ABOUT

Sex and the City, Season 2 episode 4, "They Shoot Single People Don't They."

Nagoski, E., PhD (2015). *Come as You Are: The Surprising New Science that Will Transform Your Sex Life*. Simon & Schuster.

Rodman Whiten, S. (2022, April 16). *Oral Sex On Women: What You Don't Know* [Podcast]. The Dr. Psych Mom Show.

Perel, E. *Where Should We Begin - A Game of Stories* [Game].

We're Not Really Strangers [Game].

Ma, J. (n.d.). *Erotic Blueprint Breakthrough Quiz*. https://s.pointer-pro.com/xyvvarox

CHAPTER 11. LET'S TALK ABOUT SEX (AGAIN): WHAT REALLY MATTERS IN THE BEDROOM

Sex and the City, Season 3 episode 11, "Running with Scissors."

Fein, E., & Schneider, S. (2001). *The Rules (TM): Time-Tested Secrets for Capturing the Heart of Mr. Right*. Grand Central Publishing.

Jacoby, M. (2021). *Never Waste Time on the Wrong Man Again: A 5-Step Strategic Plan to Stop Wasting Time and Finally Find "The One"*. Difference Press.

@vanessaandxander

Lehmiller, J. (2022, May 24). *The Psychology Behind Forced Sex Fantasies* [Podcast]. Sex and Psychology Podcast. https://www.sexandpsychology.com/podcasts/

Foster, E. (Creator). *Nobody Wants This* [Series].

Wiseman, J. (1996). *SM 101: A Realistic Introduction*. Greenery Press.

Miller, P. (2002). *Screw the Roses. Send Me the Thorns: The Romance and Sexual Sorcery of Sadomasochism*. Mystic Rose Books.

CHAPTER 12. PORNOGRAPHY:
THE TRUTH ABOUT THE IMPACT ON RELATIONSHIPS

Sex and the City, Season 2 episode 6, "The Cheating Curve."

Irizarry R, Gallaher H, Samuel S, Soares J, Villela J. How the Rise of Problematic Pornography Consumption and the COVID-19 Pandemic Has Led to a Decrease in Physical Sexual Interactions and Relationships and an Increase in Addictive Behaviors and Cluster B Personality Traits: A Meta-Analysis. *Cureus*. 2023 Jun 16;15(6):e40539. doi: 10.7759/cureus.40539. PMID: 37342297; PMCID: PMC10277752.

Rodman Whiten, S. (2022, August 28). Porn Use And Marriage [Podcast]. *The Dr. Psych Mom Show*. https://podtail.com/podcast/the-dr-psych-mom-show/porn-use-and-marriage/

Ogas, O., & Gaddam, S. (2011). *A Billion Wicked Thoughts: What the World's Largest Experiment Reveals about Human Desire*. Dutton.

CHAPTER 13. LOVE LANGUAGES:
THE KEY TO STRONGER CONNECTIONS

Sex and the City, Season 3 episode 4, "boy, girl, boy, girl."

Chapman, G. (1995). *The Five Love Languages: How to Express Heartfelt Commitment to Your Mate.* Northfield Publishing.

Fray, M. (2016, January 25). She Divorced Me Because I Left Dishes By The Sink. *Huff Post.*

Vanderpump, L. (Executive Producer). The Valley [Series]. Bravo. *(gives good insight into functional/dysfunctional couples)*

CHAPTER 14. GETTING SERIOUS:
BUILDING A RELATIONSHIP THAT LASTS

Sex and the City, Season 6 episode 17, "The Cold War."

Coelen, C. (Director). (2020-). *Love is Blind* [Series]. Kinetic Content.

Hendrix, H., PhD, & Hunt, H. L., PhD (2019). *Getting the Love You Want: A Guide for Couples.* St. Martin's Griffin.

Easton, D., & Hardy, J. (1997). *The Ethical Slut: A Guide to Infinite Sexual Possibilities.* Greenery Press.

Rickert, E., Samaran, N., & Fern, J. (2020). *Polysecure: Attachment, Trauma and Consensual Nonmonogamy.* Thornapple Press.

CHAPTER 15. BREAKING UP DONE RIGHT:
HOW TO END THINGS WITH RESPECT AND CARE

Sex and The City, Season 6, episode 7, "The Post-It Always Sticks Twice."

CHAPTER 16. ALL THINGS EX-WIFE, PARENTING, AND CO-PARENTING:
MANAGING LIFE AFTER DIVORCE

Sex and the City, Season 6 episode 3, "The Perfect Present."

Rodman, S. (2015). *How to Talk to Your Kids about Your Divorce: Healthy, Effective Communication Techniques for Your Changing Family.* Adams Media.

Ricci, I., PhD (1997). *Mom's House, Dad's House: Making two homes for your child.* Touchstone.

Brodesser-Akner, T. (Creator). *Fleishman Is in Trouble* [Miniseries]. FX on Hulu.

@MichelleDempsy

@nycdivorcelawyer

CONCLUSION

Sex and the City, Season 6 episode 20, "An American Girl in Paris, Part Deux" (Series Finale).

ADDITIONAL READING/CONTENT NOT SPECIFICALLY REFERENCED

Orlov, M. (1997). *The ADHD Effect on Marriage: Understand and Rebuild Your Relationship in Six Steps.* Specialty Press/A.D.D. Warehouse.

Siegel, D. J., MD, & Hartzell, M. (2013). *Parenting from the Inside Out: How a Deeper Self-Understanding Can Help You Raise Children Who Thrive.* TarcherPerigee.

Faber, A., & Mazlish, E. (2004). *How to Talk So Kids Will Listen & Listen So Kids Will Talk*. Harper Perennial.

Wong, A. Single Lady [Special]. Netflix.

SO, YOUR WIFE LEFT YOU... NOW WHAT?

ACKNOWLEDGEMENTS

I'm so incredibly lucky to have so many people to thank here.

My clients, who I dedicated this book to, for being so open and inspiring to me. You are doing the hard work of introspection and growth, and I learn so much from you. You are always motivating me to learn more and continue to grow as a therapist and human.

My family. Thanks for rallying around me during super hard times—always, but especially in the last few years. Thanks for loving Sidney to the moon and always wanting what is best for him. Mom, thanks for modeling what a successful, creative, driven, smart, beautiful divorced mom can do. Thank you for showing me it's possible to follow my passion. I guess this relationship stuff is in the blood. Jim, thanks for your calm and patient presence, and being on my team. Dad, thanks for being my cheerleader and helping me problem-solve life's challenges. Thanks for letting me vent and for the words of affirmation. Thanks to my brother, Adam, for teaching me acceptance.

Thank you to my tribe of girlfriends. My chosen family. Thanks for the cheerleading and the unwavering support. Thank you Jesse, Naomi, Lindsey, Raina, Shira. Thank you Evie for your wisdom and love, answering every "Wtf am I doing with this" text, and encouraging me to "just keep going".

Thank you to my friends and colleagues that I made throughout my training and career to this point. Never would have gotten though any of that without you. Thank you to those of you who are in the private practice trenches with me, figuring out all this (special shoutout to "therapy queens" and "PP gospel").

Thank you to my friends and colleagues who read all or parts of this book and ESPECIALLY to those who wrote endorsements: CJ and Kori. Thank you for believing in me and what I have to offer. Thank you to Natasha for your endorsement and for doing the brilliant work you do with divorced couples! So necessary. It was lovely to reconnect on this.

Thank you James Sexton, for your endorsement and your brilliant content.

Thank you to Regina DeMeo, for reading the book and making brilliant suggestions throughout the writing process, and of course for writing the forward. Your wisdom and experience was so helpful.

Thank you to the men I have met in my personal life that also inspired this project and supported me. I've made some true friends in my own journey.

Thank you to my own therapist, who encouraged me from day one to go out on my own, find my voice, explore creative endeavors, and not get in my own way.

Thank you to Lil and the folks at GWN Publishing, who loved this book idea and kept me on track, while giving me a lot of suggestions and laughs along the way, and making this actually happen. Thank you Kat, who was a huge cheerleader as well and reminded me that what I'm doing is important.

Acknowledgements

Thank you to Elliott O'Donovan, the amazingly talented photographer who took the cover and bio photos.

Thank you to the brilliant *Sex and the City* writers, and though it feels silly to thank fictional characters- thank you to Carrie, Miranda, Charlotte, and Samantha. I love you all dearly, and I am definitely some of all of you.

And of course, thank you to the best kiddo around, Sidney. Being your mom is the biggest privilege I could have dreamt of. Thank you for teaching me so much, and being my biggest inspiration to live a valued life. I hope you are always authentic and brave, especially when it is scary.

ABOUT THE AUTHOR

ELANA HOFFMAN grew up in Bethesda, MD. She attended under-graduate and graduate school at the University of Maryland College Park and is now a Licensed Clinical Psychologist with a private practice in Washington, D.C.

She, of course, specializes in relationships! She spends most of her time seeing clients, working on her practice, and parenting her kiddo. Outside of that, she's exploring all that D.C. has to offer, spending time with friends and family, practicing yoga, reading, and sometimes navigating the D.C. dating scene herself.

You can find her on Instagram @dr.elanahoffman. Her website is drelanahoffman.com, and email at drelanahoffman@gmail. com

www.ingramcontent.com/pod-product-compliance
Lightning Source LLC
Chambersburg PA
CBHW060923120626
46557CB00003B/860